Praise for *High Performance Web Sites*

"If everyone would implement just 20% of Steve's guidelines, the Web would be a dramatically better place. Between this book and Steve's YSlow extension, there's really no excuse for having a sluggish web site anymore."

—Joe Hewitt, Developer of Firebug debugger and Mozilla's DOM Inspector

"Steve Souders has done a fantastic job of distilling a massive, semi-arcane art down to a set of concise, actionable, pragmatic engineering steps that will change the world of web performance."

—Eric Lawrence, Developer of the Fiddler Web Debugger, Microsoft Corporation

"As the stress and performance test lead for Zillow.com, I have been talking to all of the developers and operations folks to get them on board with the rules Steve outlined in this book, and they all ask how they can get a hold of this book. I think this should be a mandatory read for all new UE developers and performance engineers here."

—Nate Moch, *www.zillow.com*

"*High Performance Web Sites* is an essential guide for every web developer. Steve offers straightforward, useful advice for making virtually any site noticeably faster."

—Tony Chor, Group Program Manager, Internet Explorer team, Microsoft Corporation

High Performance Web Sites

High Performance Web Sites

Essential Knowledge for Frontend Engineers

Steve Souders

O'REILLY®

Beijing • Cambridge • Farnham • Köln • Sebastopol • Taipei • Tokyo

High Performance Web Sites
by Steve Souders

Printed in the United States of America.

Published by O'Reilly Media, Inc., 1005 Gravenstein Highway North, Sebastopol, CA 95472.

O'Reilly books may be purchased for educational, business, or sales promotional use. Online editions are also available for most titles (*safari.oreilly.com*). For more information, contact our corporate/institutional sales department: (800) 998-9938 or *corporate@oreilly.com*.

Editor: Andy Oram
Production Editor: Marlowe Shaeffer
Copyeditor: Amy Thomson
Proofreader: Marlowe Shaeffer
Indexer: Julie Hawks
Cover Designer: Hanna Dyer
Interior Designer: David Futato
Illustrator: Robert Romano

Printing History:

September 2007: First Edition.

This book uses RepKover™, a durable and flexible lay-flat binding.

ISBN: 978-0-596-52930-7
[M] 42.5# [11/08]

Table of Contents

Foreword

You're lucky to be holding this book. More importantly, your web site's *users* are lucky. Implement even a few of the 14 techniques Steve shares in this groundbreaking book and your site will be faster immediately. Your users will thank you.

Here is why it matters. As a frontend engineer, you hold a tremendous amount of power and responsibility. You're the users' last line of defense. The decisions you make directly shape their experience. I believe our number one job is to take care of them and to give them what they want—quickly. This book is a toolbox to create happy users (and bosses, too). Best of all, once you put these techniques in place—in most cases, a one-time tweak—you'll be reaping the rewards far into the future.

This book will change your approach to performance optimization. When Steve began researching performance for our Platform Engineering group at Yahoo!, I believed performance was mainly a backend issue. But he showed that frontend issues account for 80% of total time. I thought frontend performance was about optimizing images and keeping CSS and JavaScript external, but the 176 pages and 14 rules you're holding in your hand right now are proof that it's much more.

I've applied his findings to several sites. Watching already-fast sites render nearly twice as quickly is tremendous. His methodology is sound, his data valid and extensive, and his findings compelling and impactful.

The discipline of frontend engineering is still young, but the book in your hands is an important step in the maturation of our craft. Together we'll raise expectations about the Web by creating better and faster (and therefore more enjoyable) interfaces and experiences.

Cheers to faster surfing!

—Nate Koechley
Senior Frontend Engineer
Yahoo! User Interface (YUI) Team, Platform Engineering, Yahoo! Inc.
San Francisco, August, 2007

Preface

In eighth grade, my history class studied the efficiency experts of the Industrial Revolution. I was enthralled by the techniques they used to identify and overcome bottlenecks in manufacturing. The most elegant improvement, in my mind, was the adjustable stepstool that afforded workers of different heights the ability to more easily reach the conveyor belt—a simple investment that resulted in improved performance for the life of the process.

Three decades later, I enjoy comparing the best practices in this book to that 19th-century stepstool. These best practices enhance an existing process. They require some upfront investment, but the cost is small—especially in comparison to the gains. And once these improvements are put in place, they continue to boost performance over the life of the development process. I hope you'll find these rules for building high performance web sites to be elegant improvements that benefit you and your users.

How This Book Is Organized

After two quick introductory chapters, I jump into the main part of this book: the 14 performance rules. Each rule is described, one per chapter, in priority order. Not every rule applies to every site, and not every site should apply a rule the same way, but each is worth considering. The final chapter of this book shows how to analyze web pages from a performance perspective, including some case studies.

Chapter A, *The Importance of Frontend Performance* explains that at least 80 percent of the time it takes to display a web page happens after the HTML document has been downloaded, and describes the importance of the techniques in this book.

Chapter B, *HTTP Overview* provides a short description of HTTP, highlighting the parts that are relevant to performance.

Chapter 1, *Rule 1: Make Fewer HTTP Requests* describes why extra HTTP requests have the biggest impact on performance, and discusses ways to reduce these HTTP requests including image maps, CSS sprites, inline images using `data:` URLs, and combining scripts and stylesheets.

Chapter 2, *Rule 2: Use a Content Delivery Network* highlights the advantages of using a content delivery network.

Chapter 3, *Rule 3: Add an Expires Header* digs into how a simple HTTP header dramatically improves your web pages by using the browser's cache.

Chapter 4, *Rule 4: Gzip Components* explains how compression works and how to enable it for your web servers, and discusses some of the compatibility issues that exist today.

Chapter 5, *Rule 5: Put Stylesheets at the Top* reveals how stylesheets affect the rendering of your page.

Chapter 6, *Rule 6: Put Scripts at the Bottom* shows how scripts affect rendering and downloading in the browser.

Chapter 7, *Rule 7: Avoid CSS Expressions* discusses the use of CSS expressions and the importance of quantifying their impact.

Chapter 8, *Rule 8: Make JavaScript and CSS External* talks about the tradeoffs of inlining your JavaScript and CSS versus putting them in external files.

Chapter 9, *Rule 9: Reduce DNS Lookups* highlights the often-overlooked impact of resolving domain names.

Chapter 10, *Rule 10: Minify JavaScript* quantifies the benefits of removing whitespace from your JavaScript.

Chapter 11, *Rule 11: Avoid Redirects* warns against using redirects, and provides alternatives that you can use instead.

Chapter 12, *Rule 12: Remove Duplicate Scripts* reveals what happens if a script is included twice in a page.

Chapter 13, *Rule 13: Configure ETags* describes how ETags work and why the default implementation is bad for anyone with more than one web server.

Chapter 14, *Rule 14: Make Ajax Cacheable* emphasizes the importance of keeping these performance rules in mind when using Ajax.

Chapter 15, *Deconstructing 10 Top Sites* gives examples of how to identify performance improvements in real-world web sites.

Conventions Used in This Book

The following typographical conventions are used in this book:

Italic
: Indicates new terms, URLs, email addresses, filenames, file extensions, pathnames, directories, Unix utilities, and general emphasis.

`Constant width`
: Indicates computer code in a broad sense. This includes commands, options, switches, variables, attributes, keys, functions, types, classes, namespaces, methods, modules, properties, parameters, values, objects, events, event handlers, XML tags, HTML tags, macros, the contents of files, and the output from commands.

HTTP requests and responses are designated graphically as shown in the following example.

`GET / HTTP/1.1 is an HTTP request header`

`HTTP/1.1 200 OK is an HTTP response header`

Code Examples

Online examples can be found on this book's companion web site:

http://stevesouders.com/hpws

Examples are included in each chapter in the context in which they are discussed. They are also listed here for easy review.

No Image Map (Chapter 1)
: *http://stevesouders.com/hpws/imagemap-no.php*

Image Map (Chapter 1)
: *http://stevesouders.com/hpws/imagemap.php*

CSS Sprites (Chapter 1)
: *http://stevesouders.com/hpws/sprites.php*

Inline Images (Chapter 1)
: *http://stevesouders.com/hpws/inline-images.php*

Inline CSS Images (Chapter 1)
: *http://stevesouders.com/hpws/inline-css-images.php*

Separate Scripts (Chapter 1)
: *http://stevesouders.com/hpws/combo-none.php*

Combined Scripts (Chapter 1)
http://stevesouders.com/hpws/combo.php

CDN (Chapter 2)
http://stevesouders.com/hpws/ex-cdn.php

No CDN (Chapter 2)
http://stevesouders.com/hpws/ex-nocdn.php

No Expires (Chapter 3)
http://stevesouders.com/hpws/expiresoff.php

Far Future Expires (Chapter 3)
http://stevesouders.com/hpws/expireson.php

Nothing Gzipped (Chapter 4)
http://stevesouders.com/hpws/nogzip.html

HTML Gzipped (Chapter 4)
http://stevesouders.com/hpws/gzip-html.html

Everything Gzipped (Chapter 4)
http://stevesouders.com/hpws/gzip-all.html

CSS at the Bottom (Chapter 5)
http://stevesouders.com/hpws/css-bottom.php

CSS at the Top (Chapter 5)
http://stevesouders.com/hpws/css-top.php

CSS at the Top Using @import (Chapter 5)
http://stevesouders.com/hpws/css-top-import.php

CSS Flash of Unstyled Content (Chapter 5)
http://stevesouders.com/hpws/css-fouc.php

Scripts in the Middle (Chapter 6)
http://stevesouders.com/hpws/js-middle.php

Scripts Block Downloads (Chapter 6)
http://stevesouders.com/hpws/js-blocking.php

Scripts at the Top (Chapter 6)
http://stevesouders.com/hpws/js-top.php

Scripts at the Bottom (Chapter 6)
http://stevesouders.com/hpws/js-bottom.php

Scripts Top vs. Bottom (Chapter 6)
http://stevesouders.com/hpws/move-scripts.php

Deferred Scripts (Chapter 6)
http://stevesouders.com/hpws/js-defer.php

Expression Counter (Chapter 7)
http://stevesouders.com/hpws/expression-counter.php

One-Time Expressions (Chapter 7)
http://stevesouders.com/hpws/onetime-expressions.php

Event Handler (Chapter 7)
http://stevesouders.com/hpws/event-handler.php

Inlined JS and CSS (Chapter 8)
http://stevesouders.com/hpws/inlined.php

External JS and CSS (Chapter 8)
http://stevesouders.com/hpws/external.php

Cacheable External JS and CSS (Chapter 8)
http://stevesouders.com/hpws/external-cacheable.php

Post-Onload Download (Chapter 8)
http://stevesouders.com/hpws/post-onload.php

Dynamic Inlining (Chapter 8)
http://stevesouders.com/hpws/dynamic-inlining.php

Small Script Normal (Chapter 10)
http://stevesouders.com/hpws/js-small-normal.php

Small Script Minified (Chapter 10)
http://stevesouders.com/hpws/js-small-minify.php

Small Script Obfuscated (Chapter 10)
http://stevesouders.com/hpws/js-small-obfuscate.php

Large Script Normal (Chapter 10)
http://stevesouders.com/hpws/js-large-normal.php

Large Script Minified (Chapter 10)
http://stevesouders.com/hpws/js-large-minify.php

Large Script Obfuscated (Chapter 10)
http://stevesouders.com/hpws/js-large-obfuscate.php

XMLHttpRequest Beacon (Chapter 11)
http://stevesouders.com/hpws/xhr-beacon.php

Image Beacon (Chapter 11)
http://stevesouders.com/hpws/redir-beacon.php

Duplicate Scripts—Not Cached (Chapter 12)
http://stevesouders.com/hpws/dupe-scripts.php

Duplicate Scripts—Cached (Chapter 12)
http://stevesouders.com/hpws/dupe-scripts-cached.php

Duplicate Scripts—10 Cached (Chapter 12)
http://stevesouders.com/hpws/dupe-scripts-cached10.php

In general, you may use the code in this book and these online examples in your programs and documentation. You do not need to contact us for permission unless you're reproducing a significant portion of the code. For example, writing a program that uses several chunks of code from this book does not require permission. Selling or distributing a CD-ROM of examples from O'Reilly books *does* require permission. Answering a question by citing this book and quoting example code does not require permission. Incorporating a significant amount of example code from this book into your product's documentation *does* require permission.

We appreciate, but do not require, attribution. An attribution usually includes the title, author, publisher, and ISBN. For example: "*High Performance Web Sites* by Steve Souders. Copyright 2007 Steve Souders, 978-0-596-52930-7."

If you feel your use of code examples falls outside fair use or the permission given above, feel free to contact us at *permissions@oreilly.com*.

Comments and Questions

Please address comments and questions concerning this book to the publisher:

O'Reilly Media, Inc.
1005 Gravenstein Highway North
Sebastopol, CA 95472
800-998-9938 (in the United States or Canada)
707-829-0515 (international or local)
707-829-0104 (fax)

We have a web page for this book, where we list errata and any additional information. You can access this page at:

http://www.oreilly.com/catalog/9780596529307

To comment or ask technical questions about this book, send email to:

bookquestions@oreilly.com

For more information about our books, conferences, Resource Centers, and the O'Reilly Network, see our web site at:

http://www.oreilly.com

Safari® Books Online

When you see a Safari® Books Online icon on the cover of your favorite technology book, that means the book is available online through the O'Reilly Network Safari Bookshelf.

Safari offers a solution that's better than e-books. It's a virtual library that lets you easily search thousands of top tech books, cut and paste code samples, download chapters, and find quick answers when you need the most accurate, current information. Try it for free at *http://safari.oreilly.com*.

Acknowledgments

Ash Patel and Geoff Ralston were the Yahoo! executives who asked me to start a center of expertise focused on performance. Several Yahoo!s helped answer questions and discuss ideas: Ryan Troll, Doug Crockford, Nate Koechley, Mark Nottingham, Cal Henderson, Don Vail, and Tenni Theurer. Andy Oram, my editor, struck the balance of patience and prodding necessary for a first-time author. Several people helped review the book: Doug Crockford, Havi Hoffman, Cal Henderson, Don Knuth, and especially Jeffrey Friedl, Alexander Kirk, and Eric Lawrence.

This book was completed predominantly in spare hours on the weekends and late at night. I thank my wife and daughters for giving me those hours on the weekends to work. I thank my parents for giving me the work ethic to do the late-night hours.

CHAPTER A

The Importance of Frontend Performance

Most of my web career has been spent as a backend engineer. As such, I dutifully approached each performance project as an exercise in backend optimization, concentrating on compiler options, database indexes, memory management, etc. There's a lot of attention and many books devoted to optimizing performance in these areas, so that's where most people spend time looking for improvements. In reality, for most web pages, less than 10–20% of the end user response time is spent getting the HTML document from the web server to the browser. If you want to dramatically reduce the response times of your web pages, you have to focus on the other 80–90% of the end user experience. What is that 80–90% spent on? How can it be reduced? The chapters that follow lay the groundwork for understanding today's web pages and provide 14 rules for making them faster.

Tracking Web Page Performance

In order to know what to improve, we need to know where the user spends her time waiting. Figure A-1 shows the HTTP traffic when Yahoo!'s home page (*http://www.yahoo.com*) is downloaded using Internet Explorer. Each bar is one HTTP request. The first bar, labeled `html`, is the initial request for the HTML document. The browser parses the HTML and starts downloading the components in the page. In this case, the browser's cache was empty, so all of the components had to be downloaded. The HTML document is only 5% of the total response time. The user spends most of the other 95% waiting for the components to download; she also spends a small amount of time waiting for HTML, scripts, and stylesheets to be parsed, as shown by the blank gaps between downloads.

Figure A-2 shows the same URL downloaded in Internet Explorer a second time. The HTML document is only 12% of the total response time. Most of the components don't have to be downloaded because they're already in the browser's cache.

5%
html
image
image
script
image
image
image
image
image
image
image
script
image
image
image
image
redirect
script
image
image
image
image
image
script
image
image
image
image
image
image
image
image
image
stylesheet
script

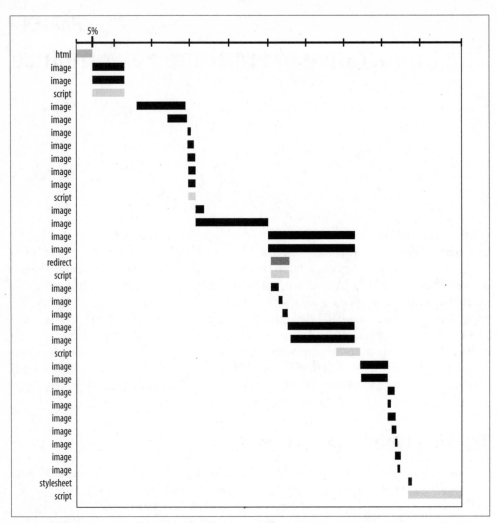

Figure A-1. Downloading http://www.yahoo.com in Internet Explorer, empty cache

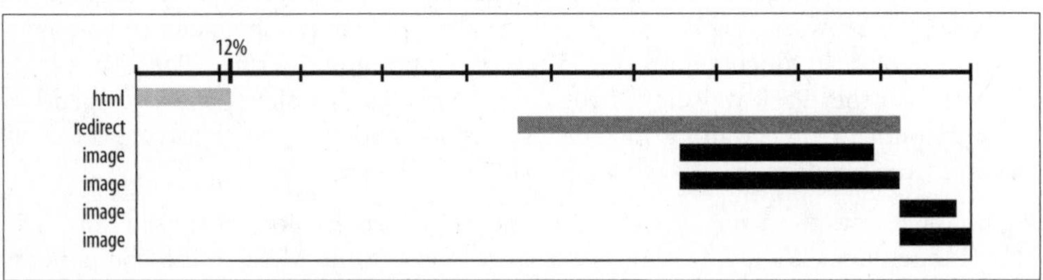

Figure A-2. Downloading http://www.yahoo.com in Internet Explorer, primed cache

Five components are requested in this second page view:

One redirect
: This redirect was downloaded previously, but the browser is requesting it again. The HTTP response's status code is 302 ("Found" or "moved temporarily") and there is no caching information in the response headers, so the browser can't cache the response. I'll discuss HTTP in Chapter B.

Three uncached images
: The next three requests are for images that were not downloaded in the initial page view. These are images for news photos and ads that change frequently.

One cached image
: The last HTTP request is a *conditional GET request*. The image is cached, but because of the HTTP response headers, the browser has to check that the image is up-to-date before showing it to the user. Conditional GET requests are also described in Chapter B.

Where Does the Time Go?

Looking at the HTTP traffic in this way, we see that at least 80% of the end user response time is spent on the components in the page. If we dig deeper into the details of these charts, we start to see how complex the interplay between browsers and HTTP becomes. Earlier, I mentioned how the HTTP status codes and headers affect the browser's cache. In addition, we can make these observations:

- The cached scenario (Figure A-2) doesn't have as much download activity. Instead, you can see a blank space with no downloads that occurs immediately following the HTML document's HTTP request. This is time when the browser is parsing HTML, JavaScript, and CSS, and retrieving components from its cache.
- Varying numbers of HTTP requests occur in parallel. Figure A-2 has a maximum of three HTTP requests happening in parallel, whereas in Figure A-1, there are as many as six or seven simultaneous HTTP requests. This behavior is due to the number of different hostnames being used, and whether they use HTTP/1.0 or HTTP/1.1. Chapter 6 explains these issues in the section "Parallel Downloads."
- Parallel requests don't happen during requests for scripts. That's because in most situations, browsers block additional HTTP requests while they download scripts. See Chapter 6 to understand why this happens and how to use this knowledge to improve page load times.

Figuring out *exactly* where the time goes is a challenge. But it's easy to see where the time does *not* go—it does *not* go into downloading the HTML document, including any backend processing. That's why frontend performance is important.

The Performance Golden Rule

This phenomenon of spending only 10–20% of the response time downloading the HTML document is not isolated to Yahoo!'s home page. This statistic holds true for all of the Yahoo! properties I've analyzed (except for Yahoo! Search because of the small number of components in the page). Furthermore, this statistic is true across most web sites. Table A-1 shows 10 top U.S. web sites extracted from *http://www.alexa.com*. Note that all of these except AOL were in the top 10 U.S. web sites. Craigslist.org was in the top 10, but its pages have little to no images, scripts, and stylesheets, and thus was a poor example to use. So, I chose to include AOL in its place.

Table A-1. Percentage of time spent downloading the HTML document for 10 top web sites

	Empty cache	Primed cache
AOL	6%	14%
Amazon	18%	14%
CNN	19%	8%
eBay	2%	8%
Google	14%	36%
MSN	3%	5%
MySpace	4%	14%
Wikipedia	20%	12%
Yahoo!	5%	12%
YouTube	3%	5%

All of these web sites spend less than 20% of the total response time retrieving the HTML document. The one exception is Google in the primed cache scenario. This is because *http://www.google.com* had only six components, and all but one were configured to be cached by the browser. On subsequent page views, with all those components cached, the only HTTP requests were for the HTML document and an image beacon.

In any optimization effort, it's critical to profile current performance to identify where you can achieve the greatest improvements. It's clear that the place to focus is frontend performance.

First, there is more potential for improvement in focusing on the frontend. If we were able to cut backend response times in half, the end user response time would decrease only 5–10% overall. If, instead, we reduce the frontend performance by half, we would reduce overall response times by 40–45%.

Second, frontend improvements typically require less time and fewer resources. Reducing backend latency involves projects such as redesigning application architecture and code, finding and optimizing critical code paths, adding or modifying hardware, distributing databases, etc. These projects take weeks or months. Most of the frontend performance improvements described in the following chapters involve best practices, such as changing web server configuration files (Chapters 3 and 4); placing scripts and stylesheets in certain places within the page (Chapters 5 and 6); and combining images, scripts, and stylesheets (Chapter 1). These projects take hours or days—much less than the time required for most backend improvements.

Third, frontend performance tuning has been proven to work. Over 50 teams at Yahoo! have reduced their end user response times by following the best practices described here, many by 25% or more. In some cases, we've had to go beyond these rules and identify improvements more specific to the site being analyzed, but generally, it's possible to achieve a 25% or greater reduction just by following these best practices.

At the beginning of every new performance improvement project, I draw a picture like that shown in Figure A-1 and explain the *Performance Golden Rule*:

> Only 10–20% of the end user response time is spent downloading the HTML document. The other 80–90% is spent downloading all the components in the page.

The rest of this book offers precise guidelines for reducing that 80–90% of end user response time. In demonstrating this, I'll cover a wide span of technologies: HTTP headers, JavaScript, CSS, Apache, and more.

Because some of the basic aspects of HTTP are necessary to understand parts of the book, I highlight them in Chapter B.

After that come the 14 rules for faster performance, each in its own chapter. The rules are listed in general order of priority. A rule's applicability to your specific web site may vary. For example, Rule 2 is more appropriate for commercial web sites and less feasible for personal web pages. If you follow all the rules that are applicable to your web site, you'll make your pages 25–50% faster and improve the user experience. The last part of the book shows how to analyze the 10 top U.S. web sites from a performance perspective.

CHAPTER B

HTTP Overview

Before diving into the specific rules for making web pages faster, it's important to understand the parts of the HyperText Transfer Protocol (HTTP) that affect performance. HTTP is how browsers and servers communicate with each other over the Internet. The HTTP specification was coordinated by the World Wide Web Consortium (W3C) and Internet Engineering Task Force (IETF), resulting in RFC 2616. HTTP/1.1 is the most common version today, but some browsers and servers still use HTTP/1.0.

HTTP is a client/server protocol made up of requests and responses. A browser sends an HTTP request for a specific URL, and a server hosting that URL sends back an HTTP response. Like many Internet services, the protocol uses a simple, plain-text format. The types of requests are GET, POST, HEAD, PUT, DELETE, OPTIONS, and TRACE. I'm going to focus on the GET request, which is the most common.

A GET request includes a URL followed by headers. The HTTP response contains a status code, headers, and a body. The following example shows the possible HTTP headers when requesting the script *yahoo_2.0.0-b2.js*.

```
GET /us.js.yimg.com/lib/common/utils/2/yahoo_2.0.0-b2.js
HTTP/1.1
Host: us.js2.yimg.com
User-Agent: Mozilla/5.0 (...) Gecko/20061206 Firefox/1.5.0.9
```

```
HTTP/1.1 200 OK
Content-Type: application/x-javascript
Last-Modified: Wed, 22 Feb 2006 04:15:54 GMT
Content-Length: 355

var YAHOO=...
```

Compression

The size of the response is reduced using compression if both the browser and server support it. Browsers announce their support of compression using the `Accept-Encoding` header. Servers identify compressed responses using the `Content-Encoding` header.

```
GET /us.js.yimg.com/lib/common/utils/2/yahoo_2.0.0-b2.js
HTTP/1.1
Host: us.js2.yimg.com
User-Agent: Mozilla/5.0 (...) Gecko/20061206 Firefox/1.5.0.9
Accept-Encoding: gzip,deflate
```

```
HTTP/1.1 200 OK
Content-Type: application/x-javascript
Last-Modified: Wed, 22 Feb 2006 04:15:54 GMT
Content-Length: 255
Content-Encoding: gzip

^_\213^H^@^@^@^@^@^@^Cl\217\315j\3030^P\204_E\361IJ...
```

Notice how the body of the response is compressed. Chapter 4 explains how to turn on compression, and warns about edge cases that can arise due to proxy caching. The `Vary` and `Cache-Control` headers are also discussed.

Conditional GET Requests

If the browser has a copy of the component in its cache, but isn't sure whether it's still valid, a conditional GET request is made. If the cached copy is still valid, the browser uses the copy from its cache, resulting in a smaller response and a faster user experience.

Typically, the validity of the cached copy is derived from the date it was last modified. The browser knows when the component was last modified based on the `Last-Modified` header in the response (refer to the previous sample responses). It uses the `If-Modified-Since` header to send the last modified date back to the server. The browser is essentially saying, "I have a version of this resource with the following last modified date. May I just use it?"

```
GET /us.js.yimg.com/lib/common/utils/2/yahoo_2.0.0-b2.js
HTTP/1.1
Host: us.js2.yimg.com
User-Agent: Mozilla/5.0 (...) Gecko/20061206 Firefox/1.5.0.9
Accept-Encoding: gzip,deflate
If-Modified-Since: Wed, 22 Feb 2006 04:15:54 GMT
```

```
HTTP/1.1 304 Not Modified
Content-Type: application/x-javascript
Last-Modified: Wed, 22 Feb 2006 04:15:54 GMT
```

If the component has not been modified since the specified date, the server returns a "304 Not Modified" status code and skips sending the body of the response, resulting in a smaller and faster response. In HTTP/1.1 the `ETag` and `If-None-Match` headers are another way to make conditional GET requests. Both approaches are discussed in Chapter 13.

Expires

Conditional GET requests and 304 responses help pages load faster, but they still require making a roundtrip between the client and server to perform the validity check. The `Expires` header eliminates the need to check with the server by making it clear whether the browser can use its cached copy of a component.

```
HTTP/1.1 200 OK
Content-Type: application/x-javascript
Last-Modified: Wed, 22 Feb 2006 04:15:54 GMT
Expires: Wed, 05 Oct 2016 19:16:20 GMT
```

When the browser sees an `Expires` header in the response, it saves the expiration date with the component in its cache. As long as the component hasn't expired, the browser uses the cached version and avoids making any HTTP requests. Chapter 3 talks about the `Expires` and `Cache-Control` headers in more detail.

Keep-Alive

HTTP is built on top of Transmission Control Protocol (TCP). In early implementations of HTTP, each HTTP request required opening a new socket connection. This is inefficient because many HTTP requests in a web page go to the same server. For example, most requests for images in a web page all go to a common image server. *Persistent Connections* (also known as *Keep-Alive* in HTTP/1.0) was introduced to solve the inefficiency of opening and closing multiple socket connections to the same server. It lets browsers make multiple requests over a single connection. Browsers and servers use the `Connection` header to indicate Keep-Alive support. The `Connection` header looks the same in the server's response.

```
GET /us.js.yimg.com/lib/common/utils/2/yahoo_2.0.0-b2.js
HTTP/1.1
Host: us.js2.yimg.com
User-Agent: Mozilla/5.0 (...) Gecko/20061206 Firefox/1.5.0.9
Accept-Encoding: gzip,deflate
Connection: keep-alive
```

```
HTTP/1.1 200 OK
Content-Type: application/x-javascript
Last-Modified: Wed, 22 Feb 2006 04:15:54 GMT
Connection: keep-alive
```

The browser or server can close the connection by sending a `Connection: close` header. Technically, the `Connection: keep-alive` header is not required in HTTP/1.1, but most browsers and servers still include it.

Pipelining, defined in HTTP/1.1, allows for sending multiple requests over a single socket without waiting for a response. Pipelining has better performance than persistent connections. Unfortunately, pipelining is not supported in Internet Explorer (up to and including version 7), and it's turned off by default in Firefox through version 2. Until pipelining is more widely adopted, Keep-Alive is the way browsers and servers can more efficiently use socket connections for HTTP. This is even more important for HTTPS because establishing new secure socket connections is more time consuming.

There's More

This chapter contains just an overview of HTTP and focuses only on the aspects that affect performance. To learn more, read the HTTP specification (*http://www.w3.org/Protocols/rfc2616/rfc2616.html*) and *HTTP: The Definitive Guide* by David Gourley and Brian Totty (O'Reilly; *http://www.oreilly.com/catalog/httptdg*). The parts highlighted here are sufficient for understanding the best practices described in the following chapters.

CHAPTER 1

Rule 1: Make Fewer HTTP Requests

The *Performance Golden Rule*, as explained in Chapter A, reveals that only 10–20% of the end user response time involves retrieving the requested HTML document. The remaining 80–90% of the time is spent making HTTP requests for all the components (images, scripts, stylesheets, Flash, etc.) referenced in the HTML document. Thus, a simple way to improve response time is to reduce the number of components, and, in turn, reduce the number of HTTP requests.

Suggesting the idea of removing components from the page often creates tension between performance and product design. In this chapter, I describe techniques for eliminating HTTP requests while avoiding the difficult tradeoff decisions between performance and design. These techniques include using image maps, CSS sprites, inline images, and combined scripts and stylesheets. Using these techniques reduces response times of the example pages by as much as 50%.

Image Maps

In its simplest form, a hyperlink associates the destination URL with some text. A prettier alternative is to associate the hyperlink with an image, for example in navbars and buttons. If you use multiple hyperlinked images in this way, image maps may be a way to reduce the number of HTTP requests without changing the page's look and feel. An *image map* allows you to associate multiple URLs with a single image. The destination URL is chosen based on where the user clicks on the image.

Figure 1-1 shows an example of five images used in a navbar. Clicking on an image takes you to the associated link. This could be done with five separate hyperlinks, using five separate images. It's more efficient, however, to use an image map because this reduces the five HTTP requests to just one HTTP request. The response time is faster because there is less HTTP overhead.

You can try this out for yourself by visiting the following URLs. Click on each link to see the roundtrip retrieval time.

Figure 1-1. Image map candidate

No Image Map
: *http://stevesouders.com/hpws/imagemap-no.php*

Image Map
: *http://stevesouders.com/hpws/imagemap.php*

When using Internet Explorer 6.0 over DSL (~900 Kbps), the image map retrieval was *56% faster* than the retrieval for the navbar with separate images for each hyperlink (354 milliseconds versus 799 milliseconds). That's because the image map has four fewer HTTP requests.

There are two types of image maps. *Server-side image maps* submit all clicks to the same destination URL, passing along the x,y coordinates of where the user clicked. The web application maps the x,y coordinates to the appropriate action. *Client-side image maps* are more typical because they map the user's click to an action without requiring a backend application. The mapping is achieved via HTML's `MAP` tag. The HTML for converting the navbar in Figure 1-1 to an image map shows how the `MAP` tag is used:

```
<img usemap="#map1" border=0 src="/images/imagemap.gif">
<map name="map1">
  <area shape="rect" coords="0,0,31,31" href="home.html" title="Home">
  <area shape="rect" coords="36,0,66,31" href="gifts.html" title="Gifts">
  <area shape="rect" coords="71,0,101,31" href="cart.html" title="Cart">
  <area shape="rect" coords="106,0,136,31" href="settings.html" title="Settings">
  <area shape="rect" coords="141,0,171,31" href="help.html" title="Help">
</map>
```

There are drawbacks to using image maps. Defining the area coordinates of the image map, if done manually, is tedious and error-prone, and it is next to impossible for any shape other than rectangles. Creating image maps via DHTML won't work in Internet Explorer.

If you're currently using multiple images in a navbar or other hyperlinks, switching to an image map is an easy way to speed up your page.

CSS Sprites

Like image maps, *CSS sprites* allow you to combine images, but they're much more flexible. The concept reminds me of a Ouija board, where the planchette (the viewer that all participants hold on to) moves around the board stopping over different letters. To use CSS sprites, multiple images are combined into a single image, similar to the one shown in Figure 1-2. This is the "Ouija board."

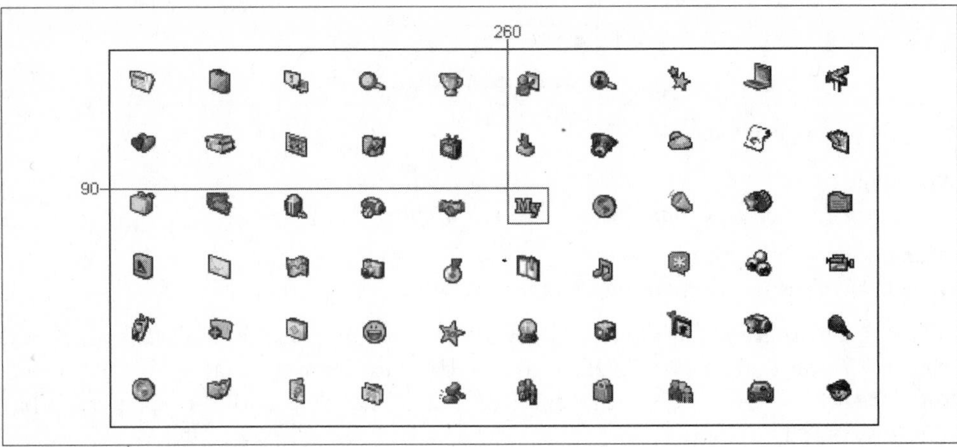

Figure 1-2. CSS sprites combine multiple images into a single image

The "planchette" is any HTML element that supports background images, such as a `SPAN` or `DIV`. The HTML element is positioned over the desired part of the background image using the CSS `background-position` property. For example, you can use the "My" icon for an element's background image as follows:

```
<div style="background-image: url('a_lot_of_sprites.gif');
            background-position: -260px -90px;
            width: 26px; height: 24px;">
</div>
```

I modified the previous image map example to use CSS sprites. The five links are contained in a `DIV` named `navbar`. Each link is wrapped around a `SPAN` that uses a single background image, `spritebg.gif`, as defined in the `#navbar span` rule. Each `SPAN` has a different class that specifies the offset into the CSS sprite using the `background-position` property:

```
<style>
#navbar span {
  width:31px;
  height:31px;
  display:inline;
  float:left;
  background-image:url(/images/spritebg.gif);
}
.home     { background-position:0 0; margin-right:4px; margin-left: 4px;}
.gifts    { background-position:-32px 0; margin-right:4px;}
.cart     { background-position:-64px 0; margin-right:4px;}
.settings { background-position:-96px 0; margin-right:4px;}
.help     { background-position:-128px 0; margin-right:0px;}
</style>

<div id="navbar" style="background-color: #F4F5EB; border: 2px ridge #333; width:
180px; height: 32px; padding: 4px 0 4px 0;">
```

```
    <a href="javascript:alert('Home')"><span class="home"></span></a>
    <a href="javascript:alert('Gifts')"><span class="gifts"></span></a>
    <a href="javascript:alert('Cart')"><span class="cart"></span></a>
    <a href="javascript:alert('Settings')"><span class="settings"></span></a>
    <a href="javascript:alert('Help')"><span class="help"></span></a>
</div>
```

It is about as fast as the image map example: 342 milliseconds versus 354 milliseconds, respectively, but this difference is too small to be significant. More importantly, it is *57% faster* than the alternative of using separate images.

CSS Sprites
http://stevesouders.com/hpws/sprites.php

Whereas the images in an image map must be contiguous, CSS sprites don't have that limitation. The many pros (and some cons) of CSS sprites are explained well in Dave Shea's authoritative web article, "CSS Sprites: Image Slicing's Kiss of Death." I touched on some of the benefits of CSS sprites already: they reduce HTTP requests by combining images and are more flexible than image maps. One surprising benefit is reduced download size. Most people would expect the combined image to be larger than the sum of the separate images because the combined image has additional area used for spacing. In fact, the combined image tends to be smaller than the sum of the separate images as a result of reducing the amount of image overhead (color tables, formatting information, etc.).

If you use a lot of images in your pages for backgrounds, buttons, navbars, links, etc., CSS sprites are an elegant solution that results in clean markup, fewer images to deal with, and faster response times.

Inline Images

It's possible to include images in your web page without any additional HTTP requests by using the `data:` URL scheme. Although this approach is not currently supported in Internet Explorer, the savings it can bring to other browsers makes it worth mentioning.

We're all familiar with URLs that include the `http:` scheme. Other schemes include the familiar `ftp:`, `file:`, and `mailto:` schemes. But there are many more schemes, such as `smtp:`, `pop:`, `dns:`, `whois:`, `finger:`, `daytime:`, `news:`, and `urn:`. Some of these are officially registered; others are accepted because of their common usage.

The `data:` URL scheme was first proposed in 1995. The specification (*http://tools.ietf.org/html/rfc2397*) says it "allows inclusion of small data items as 'immediate' data." The data is in the URL itself following this format:

```
data:[<mediatype>][;base64],<data>
```

An inline image of a red star is specified as:

```
<IMG ALT="Red Star"
SRC="data:image/gif;base64,R0lGODlhDAAMALMLAPN8ffBiYvWW
lvrKy/FvcPewsO9VVfajo+w6O/zl5estLv/8/AAAAAAAAAAAAAAACH5BAEA
AAsALAAAAAAMAAwAAAQzcElZyryTEHyTUgknHd9xGV+qKsYirKkwDYiKDBia
tt2H1KBLQRFIJAIKywRgmhwAIlEEADs=">
```

I've seen data: used only for inline images, but it can be used anywhere a URL is specified, including SCRIPT and A tags.

The main drawback of the data: URL scheme is that it's not supported in Internet Explorer (up to and including version 7). Another drawback is its possible size limitations, but Firefox 1.5 accepts inline images up to 100K. The base64 encoding increases the size of images, so the total size downloaded is increased.

The navbar from previous sections is implemented using inline images in the following example.

Inline Images
http://stevesouders.com/hpws/inline-images.php

Because data: URLs are embedded in the page, they won't be cached across different pages. You might not want to inline your company logo, because it would make every page grow by the encoded size of the logo. A clever way around this is to use CSS and inline the image as a background. Placing this CSS rule in an external stylesheet means that the data *is* cached inside the stylesheet. In the following example, the background images used for each link in the navbar are implemented using inline images in an external stylesheet.

Inline CSS Images
http://stevesouders.com/hpws/inline-css-images.php

The external stylesheet contains a rule for each SPAN that includes an inlined background image:

```
.home { background-image: url(data:image/gif;base64,R0lGODlhHwAfAPcAAAAAAIxKA...);}
.gift { background-image: url(data:image/gif;base64,R0lGODlhHwAfAPcAAAAAAABCp...);}
.cart { background-image: url(data:image/gif;base64,R0lGODlhHwAfAPcAAAAAADlCr...);}
.settings { background-image: url(data:image/gif;base64,R0lGODlhHwAfAPcAAAAAA...);}
.help { background-image: url(data:image/gif;base64,R0lGODlhHwAfAPcAAAAAALW1t...);}
```

The file_get_contents PHP function makes it easy to create inline images by reading the image from disk and inserting the contents into the page. In my example, the URL of the external stylesheet points to a PHP template: *http://stevesouders.com/hpws/inline-css-images-css.php*. The use of file_get_contents is illustrated in the PHP template that generated the stylesheet shown above:

```
.home { background-image: url(data:image/gif;base64,
   <?php echo base64_encode(file_get_contents("../images/home.gif")) ?>);}
.gift { background-image: url(data:image/gif;base64,
   <?php echo base64_encode(file_get_contents("../images/gift.gif")) ?>);}
```

```
.cart { background-image: url(data:image/gif;base64,
   <?php echo base64_encode(file_get_contents("../images/cart.gif")) ?>);}
.settings { background-image: url(data:image/gif;base64,
   <?php echo base64_encode(file_get_contents("../images/settings.gif")) ?>);}
.help { background-image: url(data:image/gif;base64,
   <?php echo base64_encode(file_get_contents("../images/help.gif")) ?>);}
```

Comparing this example to the previous examples, we see that it has about the same response time as image maps and CSS sprites, which again is more than 50% faster than the original method of having separate images for each link. Putting the inline image in an external stylesheet adds an extra HTTP request, but has the additional benefit of being cached with the stylesheet.

Combined Scripts and Stylesheets

JavaScript and CSS are used on most web sites today. Frontend engineers must choose whether to "inline" their JavaScript and CSS (i.e., embed it in the HTML document) or include it from external script and stylesheet files. In general, using external scripts and stylesheets is better for performance (this is discussed more in Chapter 8). However, if you follow the approach recommended by software engineers and modularize your code by breaking it into many small files, you decrease performance because each file results in an additional HTTP request.

Table 1-1 shows that 10 top web sites average six to seven scripts and one to two stylesheets on their home pages. These web sites were selected from *http://www.alexa.com*, as described in Chapter A. Each of these sites requires an additional HTTP request if it's not cached in the user's browser. Similar to the benefits of image maps and CSS sprites, combining these separate files into one file reduces the number of HTTP requests and improves the end user response time.

Table 1-1. Number of scripts and stylesheets for 10 top sites

Web site	Scripts	Stylesheets
http://www.amazon.com	3	1
http://www.aol.com	18	1
http://www.cnn.com	11	2
http://www.ebay.com	7	2
http://froogle.google.com	1	1
http://www.msn.com	9	1
http://www.myspace.com	2	2
http://www.wikipedia.org	3	1
http://www.yahoo.com	4	1
http://www.youtube.com	7	3

To be clear, I'm not suggesting combining scripts with stylesheets. Multiple scripts should be combined into a single script, and multiple stylesheets should be combined into a single stylesheet. In the ideal situation, there would be no more than one script and one stylesheet in each page.

The following examples show how combining scripts improves the end user response time. The page with the combined scripts loads *38% faster*. Combining stylesheets produces similar performance improvements. For the rest of this section I'll talk only about scripts (because they're used in greater numbers), but everything discussed applies equally to stylesheets.

Separate Scripts
: *http://stevesouders.com/hpws/combo-none.php*

Combined Scripts
: *http://stevesouders.com/hpws/combo.php*

For developers who have been trained to write modular code (whether in JavaScript or some other programming language), this suggestion of combining everything into a single file seems like a step backward, and indeed it would be bad in your development environment to combine all your JavaScript into a single file. One page might need `script1`, `script2`, and `script3`, while another page needs `script1`, `script3`, `script4`, and `script5`. The solution is to follow the model of compiled languages and keep the JavaScript modular while putting in place a build process for generating a target file from a set of specified modules.

It's easy to imagine a build process that includes combining scripts and stylesheets—simply concatenate the appropriate files into a single file. Combining files is easy. This step could also be an opportunity to minify the files (see Chapter 10). The difficult part can be the growth in the number of combinations. If you have a lot of pages with different module requirements, the number of combinations can be large. With 10 scripts you could have over a thousand combinations! Don't go down the path of forcing every page to have every module whether they need it or not. In my experience, a web site with many pages has a dozen or so different module combinations. It's worth the time to analyze your pages and see whether the combinatorics is manageable.

Conclusion

This chapter covered the techniques we've used at Yahoo! to reduce the number of HTTP requests in web pages without compromising the pages' design. The rules described in later chapters also present guidelines that help reduce the number of HTTP requests, but they focus primarily on subsequent page views. For components that are not critical to the initial rendering of the page, the *post-onload download* technique described in Chapter 8 helps by postponing these HTTP requests until after the page is loaded.

This chapter's rule is the one that is most effective in reducing HTTP requests for first-time visitors to your web site; that's why I put it first, and why it's the most important rule. Following its guidelines improves both first-time views and subsequent views. A fast response time on that first page view can make the difference between a user who abandons your site and one who comes back again and again.

Make fewer HTTP requests.

CHAPTER 2

Rule 2: Use a Content Delivery Network

The average user's bandwidth increases every year, but a user's proximity to your web server still has an impact on a page's response time. Web startups often have all their servers in one location. If they survive the startup phase and build a larger audience, these companies face the reality that a single server location is no longer sufficient—it's necessary to deploy content across multiple, geographically dispersed servers.

As a first step to implementing geographically dispersed content, *don't* attempt to redesign your web application to work in a distributed architecture. Depending on the application, a redesign could include daunting tasks such as synchronizing session state and replicating database transactions across server locations. Attempts to reduce the distance between users and your content could be delayed by, or never pass, this redesign step.

The correct first step is found by recalling the *Performance Golden Rule*, described in Chapter A:

> Only 10–20% of the end user response time is spent downloading the HTML document. The other 80–90% is spent downloading all the components in the page.

If the *application web servers* are closer to the user, the response time of *one* HTTP request is improved. On the other hand, if the *component web servers* are closer to the user, the response times of *many* HTTP requests are improved. Rather than starting with the difficult task of redesigning your application in order to disperse the application web servers, it's better to first disperse the component web servers. This not only achieves a bigger reduction in response times, it's also easier thanks to *content delivery networks*.

Content Delivery Networks

A content delivery network (CDN) is a collection of web servers distributed across multiple locations to deliver content to users more efficiently. This efficiency is typically discussed as a performance issue, but it can also result in cost savings. When optimizing for performance, the server selected for delivering content to a specific user is based on a measure of network proximity. For example, the CDN may choose the server with the fewest network hops or the server with the quickest response time.

Some large Internet companies own their own CDN, but it's cost effective to use a CDN service provider. Akamai Technologies, Inc. is the industry leader. In 2005, Akamai acquired Speedera Networks, the primary low-cost alternative. Mirror Image Internet, Inc. is now the leading alternative to Akamai. Limelight Networks, Inc. is another competitor. Other providers, such as SAVVIS Inc., specialize in niche markets such as video content delivery.

Table 2-1 shows 10 top Internet sites in the U.S. and the CDN service providers they use.

Table 2-1. CDN service providers used by top sites

Web site	CDN
http://www.amazon.com	Akamai
http://www.aol.com	Akamai
http://www.cnn.com	
http://www.ebay.com	Akamai, Mirror Image
http://www.google.com	
http://www.msn.com	SAVVIS
http://www.myspace.com	Akamai, Limelight
http://www.wikipedia.org	
http://www.yahoo.com	Akamai
http://www.youtube.com	

You can see that:

- Five use Akamai
- One uses Mirror Image
- One uses Limelight
- One uses SAVVIS
- Four either don't use a CDN or use a homegrown CDN solution

Smaller and noncommercial web sites might not be able to afford the cost of these CDN services. There are several free CDN services available. Globule (*http://www.globule.org*) is an Apache module developed at Vrije Universiteit in Amsterdam. CoDeeN (*http://codeen.cs.princeton.edu*) was built at Princeton University on top of PlanetLab. CoralCDN (*http://www.coralcdn.org*) is run out of New York University. They are deployed in different ways. Some require that end users configure their browsers to use a proxy. Others require developers to change the URL of their components to use a different hostname. Be wary of any that use HTTP redirects to point users to a local server, as this slows down web pages (see Chapter 11).

In addition to improved response times, CDNs bring other benefits. Their services include backups, extended storage capacity, and caching. A CDN can also help absorb spikes in traffic, for example, during times of peak weather or financial news, or during popular sporting or entertainment events.

One drawback to relying on a CDN is that your response times can be affected by traffic from other web sites, possibly even those of your competitors. A CDN service provider typically shares its web servers across all its clients. Another drawback is the occasional inconvenience of not having direct control of the content servers. For example, modifying HTTP response headers must be done through the service provider rather than directly by your ops team. Finally, if your CDN service provider's performance degrades, so does yours. In Table 2-1, you can see that eBay and MySpace each use two CDN service providers, a smart move if you want to hedge your bets.

CDNs are used to deliver static content, such as images, scripts, stylesheets, and Flash. Serving dynamic HTML pages involves specialized hosting requirements: database connections, state management, authentication, hardware and OS optimizations, etc. These complexities are beyond what a CDN provides. Static files, on the other hand, are easy to host and have few dependencies. That is why a CDN is easily leveraged to improve the response times for a geographically dispersed user population.

The Savings

The two online examples discussed in this section demonstrate the response time improvements gained from using a CDN. Both examples include the same test components: five scripts, one stylesheet, and eight images. In the first example, these components are hosted on the Akamai Technologies CDN. In the second example, they are hosted on a single web server.

CDN
: *http://stevesouders.com/hpws/ex-cdn.php*

No CDN
: *http://stevesouders.com/hpws/ex-nocdn.php*

The example with components hosted on the CDN loaded 18% faster than the page with all components hosted from a single web server (1013 milliseconds versus 1232 milliseconds). I tested this over DSL (~900 Kbps) from my home in California. Your results will vary depending on your connection speed and geographic location. The single web server is located near Washington, DC. The closer you live to Washington, DC, the less of a difference you'll see in response times in the CDN example.

If you conduct your own response time tests to gauge the benefits of using a CDN, it's important to keep in mind that the location from which you run your test has an impact on the results. For example, based on the assumption that most web companies choose a data center close to their offices, your web client at work is probably located close to your current web servers. Thus, if you run a test from your browser at work, the response times *without* using a CDN are often best case. It's important to remember that most of your users are not located that close to your web servers. To measure the true impact of switching to a CDN, you need to measure the response times from multiple geographic locations. Services such as Keynote Systems (*http://www.keynote.com*) and Gomez (*http://www.gomez.com*) are helpful for conducting such tests.

At Yahoo!, this factor threw us off for awhile. Before switching Yahoo! Shopping to Akamai, our preliminary tests were run from a lab at Yahoo! headquarters, located near a Yahoo! data center. The response time improvements gained by switching to Akamai's CDN—as measured from that lab—were less than 5% (not very impressive). We knew the response time improvements would be better when we exposed the CDN change to our live users, spread around the world. When we exposed the change to end users, there was an overall 20% reduction in response times on the Yahoo! Shopping site, just from moving all the static components to a CDN.

Use a content delivery network.

CHAPTER 3

Rule 3: Add an Expires Header

Fast response time is not your only consideration when designing web pages. If it were, then we'd all take Rule 1 to an extreme and place no images, scripts, or stylesheets in our pages. However, we all understand that images, scripts, and stylesheets can enhance the user experience, even if it means that the page will take longer to load. Rule 3, described in this chapter, shows how you can improve page performance by making sure these components are configured to maximize the browser's caching capabilities.

Today's web pages include many components and that number continues to grow. A first-time visitor to your page may have to make several HTTP requests, but by using a future `Expires` header, you make those components cacheable. This avoids unnecessary HTTP requests on subsequent page views. A future `Expires` header is most often used with images, but it should be used on *all* components, including scripts, stylesheets, and Flash. Most top web sites are not currently doing this. In this chapter, I point out these sites and show why their pages aren't as fast as they could be. Adding a future `Expires` header incurs some additional development costs, as described in the section "Revving Filenames."

Expires Header

Browsers (and proxies) use a cache to reduce the number of HTTP requests and decrease the size of HTTP responses, thus making web pages load faster. A web server uses the `Expires` header to tell the web client that it can use the current copy of a component until the specified time. The HTTP specification summarizes this header as "the date/time after which the response is considered stale." It is sent in the HTTP response.

```
Expires: Thu, 15 Apr 2010 20:00:00 GMT
```

This is a *far future Expires header*, telling the browser that this response won't be stale until April 15, 2010. If this header is returned for an image in a page, the browser uses the cached image on subsequent page views, reducing the number of HTTP requests by one. See Chapter B for a review of the Expires header and HTTP.

Max-Age and mod_expires

Before I explain how better caching improves performance, it's important to mention an alternative to the Expires header. The Cache-Control header was introduced in HTTP/1.1 to overcome limitations with the Expires header. Because the Expires header uses a specific date, it has stricter clock synchronization requirements between server and client. Also, the expiration dates have to be constantly checked, and when that future date finally arrives, a new date must be provided in the server's configuration.

Alternatively, Cache-Control uses the max-age directive to specify how long a component is cached. It defines the freshness window in seconds. If less than max-age seconds have passed since the component was requested, the browser will use the cached version, thus avoiding an additional HTTP request. A far future max-age header might set the freshness window 10 years in the future.

```
Cache-Control: max-age=315360000
```

Using Cache-Control with max-age overcomes the limitations of Expires, but you still might want an Expires header for browsers that don't support HTTP/1.1 (even though this is probably less than 1% of your traffic). You could specify both response headers, Expires and Cache-Control max-age. If both are present, the HTTP specification dictates that the max-age directive will override the Expires header. However, if you're conscientious, you'll still worry about the clock synchronization and configuration maintenance issues with Expires.

Fortunately, the mod_expires Apache module (*http://httpd.apache.org/docs/2.0/mod/mod_expires.html*) lets you use an Expires header that sets the date in a relative fashion similar to max-age. This is done via the ExpiresDefault directive. In this example, the expiration date for images, scripts, and stylesheets is set 10 years from the time of the request:

```
<FilesMatch "\.(gif|jpg|js|css)$">
  ExpiresDefault "access plus 10 years"
</FilesMatch>
```

The time can be specified in years, months, weeks, days, hours, minutes, or seconds. It sends both an Expires header and a Cache-Control max-age header in the response.

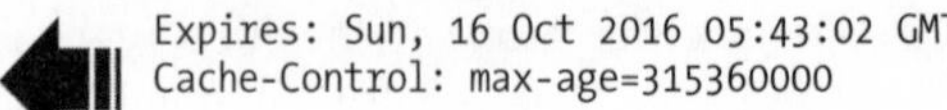

```
Expires: Sun, 16 Oct 2016 05:43:02 GMT
Cache-Control: max-age=315360000
```

The actual value for the expiration date varies depending on when the request is received, but in this case, it's always 10 years out. Since `Cache-Control` takes precedence and is expressed in seconds relative to the request, clock synchronization issues are avoided. There is no fixed date to worry about updating, and it works in HTTP/1.0 browsers. The best solution to improve caching across all browsers is to use an `Expires` header set with `ExpiresDefault`.

A survey of 10 top web sites (see Table 3-1) shows that of the seven that use these headers, five use both `Expires` and `Cache-Control max-age`. One uses only `Expires` and another uses only `Cache-Control max-age`. Sadly, three don't use either.

Table 3-1. Usage of Expires and max-age

Web site	Expires	max-age
http://www.amazon.com		
http://www.aol.com	✓	✓
http://www.cnn.com		
http://www.ebay.com	✓	✓
http://www.google.com	✓	
http://www.msn.com	✓	✓
http://www.myspace.com		✓
http://www.wikipedia.org	✓	✓
http://www.yahoo.com	✓	✓
http://www.youtube.com		

Empty Cache vs. Primed Cache

Using a far future `Expires` header affects page views only after a user has already visited your site. It has no effect on the number of HTTP requests when a user visits your site for the first time and the browser's cache is empty. Therefore, the impact of this performance improvement depends on how often users hit your pages with a primed cache. It's likely that a majority of your traffic comes from users with a primed cache. Making your components cacheable improves the response time for these users.

When I say "empty cache" or "primed cache," I mean the state of the browser's cache relative to your page. The cache is "empty" if none of your page's components are in the cache. The browser's cache might contain components from other web sites, but that doesn't help your page. Conversely, the cache is "primed" if all of your page's cacheable components are in the cache.

The number of empty versus primed cache page views depends on the nature of the web application. A site like "word of the day" might only get one page view per session from the typical user. There are several reasons why the "word of the day" components might not be in the cache the next time a user visits the site:

- Despite her desire for a better vocabulary, a user may visit the page only weekly or monthly, rather than daily.
- A user may have manually cleared her cache since her last visit.
- A user may have visited so many other web sites that her cache filled up, and the "word of the day" components were pushed out.
- The browser or an antivirus application may have cleared the cache when the browser was closed.

With only one page view per session, it's not very likely that "word of the day" components are in the cache, so the percentage of primed cache page views is low.

On the other hand, a travel or email web site might get multiple page views per user session and the number of primed cache page views is likely to be high. In this instance, more page views will find your components in the browser's cache.

We measured this at Yahoo! and found that the number of *unique users who came in at least once a day with a primed cache ranged from 40–60%*, depending on the Yahoo! property. That same study revealed that the number of *page views with a primed cache was 75–85%.*[*] Note that the first statistic measures "unique users" while the second measures "page views." The percentage of page views with a primed cache is higher than the percentage of unique users with a primed cache because many Yahoo! properties receive multiple page views per session. Users show up once during the day with an empty cache, but make several subsequent page views with a primed cache.

These browser cache statistics illustrate why it's important to optimize the primed cache experience. We want the 40–60% of users and 75–85% of page views with a primed cache to be optimized. The percentages for your site may vary, but if users typically visit your site at least once a month or have multiple page views per session, the statistics are probably similar. By using a far future `Expires` header you increase the number of components that are cached by the browser and reused on subsequent page views without sending a single byte over the user's Internet connection.

More Than Just Images

Using a far future `Expires` header on images is fairly common, but this best practice should not be limited to images. A far future `Expires` header should be included on

[*] Tenni Theurer, "Performance Research, Part 2: Browser Cache Usage – Exposed!", *http://yuiblog.com/blog/2007/01/04/performance-research-part-2*.

any component that changes infrequently, including scripts, stylesheets, and Flash components. Typically, an HTML document won't have a future `Expires` header because it contains dynamic content that is updated on each user request.

In the ideal situation, all the components in a page would have a far future `Expires` header, and subsequent page views would make just a single HTTP request for the HTML document. When all of the document's components are read from the browser's cache, the response time is cut by 50% or more.

I surveyed 10 top Internet sites in the U.S and recorded how many of the images, scripts, and stylesheets had an `Expires` or a `Cache-Control max-age` header set at least 30 days in the future. As shown in Table 3-2, the news isn't good. Three types of components are tallied: images, stylesheets, and scripts. Table 3-2 shows the number of components that are cacheable for at least 30 days out of the total number of components of each type. Let's see to what extent these sites employ the practice of making their components cacheable:

- Five sites make a majority of their *images* cacheable for 30 days or more.
- Four sites make a majority of their *stylesheets* cacheable for 30 days or more.
- Two sites make a majority of their *scripts* cacheable for 30 days or more.

Table 3-2. Components with an Expires header

Web site	Images	Stylesheets	Scripts	Median Last-Modified Δ
http://www.amazon.com	0/62	0/1	0/3	114 days
http://www.aol.com	23/43	1/1	6/18	217 days
http://www.cnn.com	0/138	0/2	2/11	227 days
http://www.ebay.com	16/20	0/2	0/7	140 days
http://froogle.google.com	1/23	0/1	0/1	454 days
http://www.msn.com	32/35	1/1	3/9	34 days
http://www.myspace.com	0/18	0/2	0/2	1 day
http://www.wikipedia.org	6/8	1/1	2/3	1 day
http://www.yahoo.com	23/23	1/1	4/4	-
http://www.youtube.com	0/32	0/3	0/7	26 days

The overall percentage from Table 3-2 indicates that 74.7% of all components were either not cacheable or were cacheable for less than 30 days. One possible explanation is that these components shouldn't be cached. For example, a news site such as *cnn.com*, with 0 out of 138 images cacheable, may have many news photos that should be constantly refreshed in case of updates, rather than cached in the user's browser. The `Last-Modified` header allows us to see when a component was last modified. If components weren't cached because they change frequently, we'd expect to see recent `Last-Modified` dates.

Table 3-2 shows the median Last-Modified delta (the difference between the current date and the Last-Modified date) for all uncached components. In the case of *cnn.com* the median Last-Modified delta is 227 days. Half of the uncached components had not been modified in over 227 days, so image freshness is not the issue here.

This was the case at Yahoo!, as well. In the past, Yahoo! did not make scripts, stylesheets, nor some images cacheable. The logic behind not caching these components was that the user should request them every time in order to get updates because they changed frequently. However, when we discovered how infrequently the files changed in practice, we realized that making them cacheable resulted in a better user experience. Yahoo! chose to make them cacheable even at the cost of additional development expense, as described in the next section.

Revving Filenames

If we configure components to be cached by browsers and proxies, how do users get updates when those components change? When an `Expires` header is present, the cached version is used until the expiration date. The browser doesn't check for any changes until after the expiration date has passed. That's why using the `Expires` header significantly reduces response times—browsers read the components straight from disk without generating any HTTP traffic. Thus, even if you update the component on your servers, users who have already been to your site will most likely not get the updated component (since the previous version is in their cache).

To ensure users get the latest version of a component, change the component's filename in all of your HTML pages. Mark Nottingham's web article "Caching Tutorial for Web Authors and Webmasters" says:

> The most effective solution is to change any links to them; that way, completely new representations will be loaded fresh from the origin server.

Depending on how you construct your HTML pages, this practice may be either trivial or painful. If you generate your HTML pages dynamically using PHP, Perl, etc., a simple solution is to use variables for all your component filenames. With this approach, updating a filename across all your pages is as simple as changing the variable in one location. At Yahoo! we often make this step part of the build process: a version number is embedded in the component's filename (for example, *yahoo_2.0.6.js*) and the revved filename is automatically updated in the global mapping. Embedding the version number not only changes the filename, it also makes it easier to find the exact source code files when debugging.

Examples

The following two examples demonstrate the performance improvement achieved by using a far future `Expires` header. Both examples include the same components: six images, three scripts, and one stylesheet. In the first example, these components do *not* have a far future `Expires` header. In the second example, they do.

No Expires
: *http://stevesouders.com/hpws/expiresoff.php*

Far Future Expires
: *http://stevesouders.com/hpws/expireson.php*

Adding the far future `Expires` header drops the response time for subsequent page views from ~600 milliseconds to ~260 milliseconds, *a 57% reduction* when tested over DSL at 900 Kbps. With more components in the page, response times improve even more. If your pages average more than six images, three scripts, and one stylesheet, your pages should show a speed up greater than the 57% I found in my example.

Where exactly do these response time savings come from? As I mentioned earlier, a component with a far future `Expires` header is cached, and on subsequent requests the browser reads it straight from disk, avoiding an HTTP request. However, I didn't describe the converse. If a component *does not* have a far future `Expires` header, it's still stored in the browser's cache. On subsequent requests the browser checks the cache and finds that the component is expired (in HTTP terms it is "stale"). For efficiency, the browser sends a *conditional GET request* to the origin server. See Chapter B for an example. If the component hasn't changed, the origin server avoids sending back the entire component and instead sends back a few headers telling the browser to use the component in its cache.

Those conditional requests add up. That's where the savings come from. Most of the time, as we saw when looking at the 10 top web sites, the component hasn't changed and the browser is going to read it from disk anyway. You can cut your response times in half by using the `Expires` header to avoid these unnecessary HTTP requests.

> **Add a far future `Expires` header to your components.**

CHAPTER 4

Rule 4: Gzip Components

The time it takes to transfer an HTTP request and response across the network can be significantly reduced by decisions made by frontend engineers. It's true that the end user's bandwidth speed, Internet service provider, proximity to peering exchange points, and other factors are beyond the control of the development team. However, there are more variables that affect response times. Rules 1 and 3 address response times by eliminating unnecessary HTTP requests. If there is no HTTP request then there is no network activity—the ideal situation. Rule 2 improves response times by bringing the HTTP response closer to the user.

Rule 4, examined in this chapter, reduces response times by reducing the size of the HTTP response. If an HTTP request results in a smaller response, the transfer time decreases because fewer packets must travel from the server to the client. This effect is even greater for slower bandwidth speeds. This chapter shows how to use gzip encoding to compress HTTP responses, and thus reduce network response times. This is the easiest technique for reducing page weight and it also has the biggest impact. There are other ways you can reduce the HTML document's page weight (strip comments and shorten URLs, for example), but they are typically less effective and require more work.

How Compression Works

The same file compression that has been used for decades to reduce file sizes in email messages and on FTP sites is also used to deliver compressed web pages to browsers. Starting with HTTP/1.1, web clients indicate support for compression with the `Accept-Encoding` header in the HTTP request.

```
Accept-Encoding: gzip, deflate
```

If the web server sees this header in the request, it may compress the response using one of the methods listed by the client. The web server notifies the web client of this via the `Content-Encoding` header in the response.

```
Content-Encoding: gzip
```

Gzip is currently the most popular and effective compression method. It is a free format (i.e., unencumbered by patents or other restrictions) developed by the GNU project and standardized by RFC 1952. The only other compression format you're likely to see is *deflate*, but it's much less popular. In fact, I have seen only one site that uses deflate: *msn.com*. Browsers that support deflate also support gzip, but several browsers that support gzip do not support deflate, so gzip is the preferred method of compression.

What to Compress

Servers choose what to gzip based on file type, but are typically too limited in what they are configured to compress. Many web sites gzip their HTML documents. It's also worthwhile to gzip your scripts and stylesheets, but many web sites miss this opportunity (in fact, it's worthwhile to compress any text response including XML and JSON, but the focus here is on scripts and stylesheets since they're the most prevalent). Image and PDF files should *not* be gzipped because they are already compressed. Trying to gzip them not only wastes CPU resources, it can also potentially increase file sizes.

There is a cost to gzipping: it takes additional CPU cycles on the server to carry out the compression and on the client to decompress the gzipped file. To determine whether the benefits outweigh the costs you would have to consider the size of the response, the bandwidth of the connection, and the Internet distance between the client and the server. This information isn't generally available, and even if it were, there would be too many variables to take into consideration. Generally, it's worth gzipping any file greater than 1 or 2K. The `mod_gzip_minimum_file_size` directive controls the minimum file size you're willing to compress. The default value is 500 bytes.

I looked at the use of gzip on 10 of the most popular U.S. web sites. Nine sites gzipped their HTML documents, seven sites gzipped *most* of their scripts and stylesheets, and only five gzipped *all* of their scripts and stylesheets. The sites that don't compress all of their HTML, stylesheets, and scripts are missing the opportunity to reduce the page weight by up to 70%, as we'll see in the next section, "The Savings." A survey of major web sites and what they choose to compress is shown in Table 4-1.

http://www.msn.com	✓	deflate	deflate
http://www.myspace.com	✓	✓	✓
http://www.wikipedia.org	✓	✓	✓
http://www.yahoo.com	✓	✓	✓
http://www.youtube.com	✓	some	some

The Savings

Gzipping generally reduces the response size by about 70%. Table 4-2 shows examples of size reductions for scripts and stylesheets (small and large). In addition to gzip, the results for deflate are also shown.

Table 4-2. Compression sizes using gzip and deflate

File type	Uncompressed size	Gzip size	Gzip savings	Deflate size	Deflate savings
Script	3,277 bytes	1076 bytes	67%	1112 bytes	66%
Script	39,713 bytes	14,488 bytes	64%	16,583 bytes	58%
Stylesheet	968 bytes	426 bytes	56%	463 bytes	52%
Stylesheet	14,122 bytes	3,748 bytes	73%	4,665 bytes	67%

It's clear from Table 4-2 why gzip is typically the choice for compression. Gzip reduces the response by about 66% overall, while deflate reduces the response by 60%. For these files, gzip compresses ~6% more than deflate.

Configuration

The module used for configuring gzip depends on your version of Apache: Apache 1.3 uses `mod_gzip` while Apache 2.x uses `mod_deflate`. This section describes how to configure each module, and focuses on Apache because it is the most popular web server on the Internet.

Apache 1.3: mod_gzip

Gzip compression for Apache 1.3 is provided by the `mod_gzip` module. There are many `mod_gzip` configuration directives, and these are described on the `mod_gzip` web site (*http://www.schroepl.net/projekte/mod_gzip*). Here are the most commonly used directives:

`mod_gzip_on`
: Enables mod_gzip.

`mod_gzip_item_include`
`mod_gzip_item_exclude`
: Define which requests to gzip or not to gzip based on file type, MIME type, user agent, etc.

Most web hosting services have `mod_gzip` turned on for `text/html` by default. The most important configuration change you should make is to explicitly compress scripts and stylesheets. You can do this using the following Apache 1.3 directives:

```
mod_gzip_item_include        file      \.js$
mod_gzip_item_include        mime      ^application/x-javascript$
mod_gzip_item_include        file      \.css$
mod_gzip_item_include        mime      ^text/css$
```

The gzip command-line utility offers an option that controls the degree of compression, trading off CPU usage for size reduction, but there is no configuration directive to control the compression level in `mod_gzip`. If the CPU load caused by streaming compression is an issue, consider caching the compressed responses, either on disk or in memory. Compressing your responses and updating the cache manually adds to your maintenance work and can become a burden. Fortunately, there are options for `mod_gzip` to automatically save the gzipped content to disk and update that gzipped content when the source changes. Use the `mod_gzip_can_negotiate` and `mod_gzip_update_static` directives to do this.

Apache 2.x: mod_deflate

Compression in Apache 2.x is done with the `mod_deflate` module. Despite the name of the module, it does compression using gzip. The basic configuration shown in the previous section for compressing scripts and stylesheets is done in one line:

```
AddOutputFilterByType DEFLATE text/html text/css application/x-javascript
```

Unlike `mod_gzip`, `mod_deflate` contains a directive for controlling the level of compression: `DeflateCompressionLevel`. For more configuration information, see the Apache 2.0 `mod_deflate` documentation at *http://httpd.apache.org/docs/2.0/mod/mod_deflate.html*.

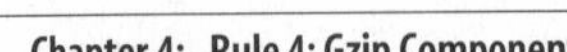

When the browser sends the request through a proxy it gets more complicated. Suppose that the first request to the proxy for a certain URL comes from a browser that *does not* support gzip. This is the first request to the proxy, so its cache is empty. The proxy forwards that request to the web server. The web server's response is uncompressed. That uncompressed response is cached by the proxy and sent on to the browser. Now, suppose the second request to the proxy for the same URL comes from a browser that *does* support gzip. The proxy responds with the (uncompressed) contents in its cache, missing the opportunity to use gzip. The situation is worse if the sequence is reversed: when the first request is from a browser that supports gzip and the second request is from a browser that doesn't. In this case, the proxy has a compressed version of the contents in its cache and serves that version to all subsequent browsers whether they support gzip or not.

The way around this problem is to add the `Vary` header in the response from your web server. The web server tells the proxy to vary the cached responses based on one or more request headers. Because the decision to compress is based on the `Accept-Encoding` request header, it makes sense to include `Accept-Encoding` in the server's `Vary` response header.

```
Vary: Accept-Encoding
```

This causes the proxy to cache multiple versions of the response, one for each value of the `Accept-Encoding` request header. In our previous example, the proxy would cache two versions of each response: the compressed content for when `Accept-Encoding` is `gzip` and the uncompressed content for when `Accept-Encoding` is not specified at all. When a browser hits the proxy with the request header `Accept-Encoding: gzip` it receives the compressed response. Browsers without an `Accept-Encoding` request header receive the uncompressed response. By default, `mod_gzip` adds the `Vary: Accept-Encoding` header to all responses to provoke the right behavior from the proxy. For more information about `Vary`, visit *http://www.w3.org/Protocols/rfc2616/rfc2616-sec14.html#sec14.44*.

Edge Cases

The coordination of compression between servers and clients seems simple, but it must work correctly. The page could easily break if either the client or server makes a mistake (sending gzipped content to a client that can't understand it, forgetting to declare a compressed response as gzip-encoded, etc.). Mistakes don't happen often, but there are *edge cases* to take into consideration.

Approximately 90% of today's Internet traffic travels through browsers that claim to support gzip. If a browser says it supports gzip you can generally trust it. There are some known bugs with unpatched early versions of Internet Explorer, specifically Internet Explorer 5.5 and Internet Explorer 6.0 SP1, and Microsoft has published two Knowledge Base articles documenting the problem (*http://support.microsoft.com/kb/313712/en-us* and *http://support.microsoft.com/kb/312496/en-us*). There are other known problems, but they occur on browsers that represent less than 1% of Internet traffic. A safe approach is to serve compressed content only for browsers that are proven to support it, such as Internet Explorer 6.0 and later and Mozilla 5.0 and later. This is called a *browser whitelist* approach.

With this approach you may miss the opportunity to serve compressed content to a few browsers that would have supported it. The alternative—serving compressed content to a browser that *can't* support it—is far worse. Using `mod_gzip` in Apache 1.3, a browser whitelist is specified using `mod_gzip_item_include` with the appropriate `User-Agent` values:

```
mod_gzip_item_include reqheader "User-Agent: MSIE [6-9]"
mod_gzip_item_include reqheader "User-Agent: Mozilla/[5-9]"
```

In Apache 2.x use the `BrowserMatch` directive:

```
BrowserMatch ^MSIE [6-9] gzip
BrowserMatch ^Mozilla/[5-9] gzip
```

Adding proxy caches to the mix complicates the handling of these edge case browsers. It's not possible to share your browser whitelist configuration with the proxy. The directives used to set up the browser whitelist are too complex to encode using HTTP headers. The best you can do is add `User-Agent` to the `Vary` header as another criterion for the proxy.

```
Vary: Accept-Encoding,User-Agent
```

Once again, `mod_gzip` takes care of this automatically by adding the `User-Agent` field to the `Vary` header when it detects that you're using a browser whitelist. Unfortunately, there are thousands of different values for `User-Agent`. It's unlikely that the proxy is able to cache all the combinations of `Accept-Encoding` and `User-Agent` for all the URLs it proxies. The `mod_gzip` documentation (*http://www.schroepl.net/projekte/*

bandwidth costs because proxies won't cache your content.

This decision about how to balance between compression and proxy support is complex, trading off fast response times, reduced bandwidth costs, and edge case browser bugs. The right answer for you depends on your site:

- If your site has few users and they're a niche audience (for example, an intranet or all using Firefox 1.5), edge case browsers are less of a concern. Compress your content and use `Vary: Accept-Encoding`. This improves the user experience by reducing the size of components and leveraging proxy caches.
- If you're watching bandwidth costs closely, do the same as in the previous case: compress your content and use `Vary: Accept-Encoding`. This reduces the bandwidth costs from your servers and increases the number of requests handled by proxies.
- If you have a large, diverse audience, can afford higher bandwidth costs, and have a reputation for high quality, compress your content and use `Cache-Control: Private`. This disables proxies but avoids edge case bugs.

There is one more proxy edge case worth pointing out. The problem is that, by default, ETags (explained in Chapter 13) don't reflect whether the content is compressed, so proxies might serve the wrong content to a browser. The issue is described in Apache's bug database (*http://issues.apache.org/bugzilla/show_bug.cgi?id=39727*). The best solution is to disable ETags. Since that's also the solution proposed in Chapter 13, I go into more detail about ETags there.

Gzip in Action

Three examples for Rule 4 demonstrate the different degrees of compression you can deploy across your site.

Nothing Gzipped
: *http://stevesouders.com/hpws/nogzip.html*

HTML Gzipped
: *http://stevesouders.com/hpws/gzip-html.html*

Everything Gzipped
: *http://stevesouders.com/hpws/gzip-all.html*

In addition to the 48.6K HTML document, each example page contains a 59.9K stylesheet and a 68.0K script. Table 4-3 shows how the total page size varies with the amount of compression that is performed. Compressing the HTML document, stylesheet, and script reduces this page size from 177.6K to 46.4K, *a size reduction of 73.8%!* Compression typically reduces the content size by approximately 70%, but it varies depending on the amount of whitespace and character repetition.

Table 4-3. Page weight savings for different levels of compression

Example	Components (HTML, CSS, JS)	Total size	Size savings	Response time	Time savings
Nothing Gzipped	48.6K, 59.9K, 68.0K	177.6K	-	1562 ms	-
HTML Gzipped	13.9K, 59.9K, 68.0K	141.9K	34.7K (19.7%)	1411 ms	151 ms (9.7%)
Everything Gzipped	13.9K, 14.4K, 18.0K	46.4K	130.2K (73.8%)	731 ms	831 ms (53.2%)

The page with everything compressed loads ~831 milliseconds faster than the non-compressed example, *a response time reduction of 53.2%*. This was measured over a 900 Kbps DSL line. The absolute response time values vary depending on Internet connection, CPU, browser, geographic location, etc. However, the relative savings remain about the same. A simple change in your web server configuration, compressing as many components as possible, dramatically improves the speed of your web pages.

Gzip your scripts and stylesheets.

A team running a major portal at Yahoo! added several DHTML features to their page while trying to ensure there was no adverse effect on response times. One of the more complex DHTML features, a pop-up `DIV` for sending email messages, was not part of the actual rendering of the page—it was accessible only after the page had loaded and the user clicked on the button to send the email message. Since it wasn't used to render the page, the frontend engineer put the CSS for the pop-up `DIV` in an external stylesheet and added the corresponding `LINK` tag at the bottom of the page with the expectation that including it at the end would make the page load faster.

The logic behind this made sense. Many other components (images, stylesheets, scripts, etc.) were required to render the page. Since components are (in general) downloaded in the order in which they appear in the document, putting the DHTML feature's stylesheet last would allow the more critical components to be downloaded first, resulting in a faster-loading page.

Or would it?

In Internet Explorer (still the most popular browser) the resulting page was noticeably slower than the old design. While trying to find ways to speed up the page, we discovered that moving the DHTML feature's stylesheet to the top of the document, in the `HEAD`, made the page load faster. This contradicted what we expected. How could putting the stylesheet first, thus delaying the critical components in the page, actually improve the page load time? Further investigation led to the creation of Rule 5.

Progressive Rendering

Frontend engineers who care about performance want a page to load progressively; that is, we want the browser to display whatever content it has as soon as possible. This is especially important for pages with a lot of content and for users on slower Internet connections. The importance of giving users visual feedback has been well researched and documented. In his web article,* Jakob Nielson, pioneering usability engineer, stresses the importance of visual feedback in terms of a progress indicator.

> Progress indicators have three main advantages: They reassure the user that the system has not crashed but is working on his or her problem; they indicate approximately how long the user can be expected to wait, thus allowing the user to do other activities during long waits; and they finally provide something for the user to look at, thus making the wait less painful. This latter advantage should not be underestimated and is one reason for recommending a graphic progress bar instead of just stating the expected remaining time in numbers.

In our case the HTML page *is* the progress indicator. When the browser loads the page progressively, the header, the navigation bar, the logo at the top, etc. all serve as visual feedback for the user who is waiting for the page. This improves the overall user experience.

The problem with putting stylesheets near the bottom of the document is that it prohibits progressive rendering in many browsers. Browsers block rendering to avoid having to redraw elements of the page if their styles change. Rule 5 has less to do with the actual time to load the page's components and more to do with how the browser reacts to the order of those components. In fact, the page that *feels slower* is ironically the page that loads the visible components *faster*. The browser delays showing any visible components while it and the user wait for the stylesheet at the bottom. The examples in the following section demonstrate this phenomenon, which I call the "blank white screen."

sleep.cgi

While building the examples of this phenomenon, I developed a tool that I've found extremely useful for showing how delayed components affect web pages: *sleep.cgi*. It's a simple Perl CGI program that takes the following parameters:

`sleep`
: How long (in seconds) the response should be delayed. The default is `0`.

`type`
: The type of component to return. Possible values are `gif`, `js`, `css`, `html`, and `swf`. The default value is `gif`.

`expires`
: One of three values: `-1` (returns an `Expires` header in the past), `0` (no `Expires` header is returned), and `1` (returns an `Expires` header in the future). The default is `1`.

* Jakob Nielson, "Response Times: The Three Important Limits," *http://www.useit.com/papers/responsetime.html*.

slow images and a slow stylesheet. Those are achieved with the following requests to *sleep.cgi*:

```
<img src="/bin/sleep.cgi?type=gif&sleep=2&expires=-1&last=0">
<link rel="stylesheet" href="/bin/sleep.cgi?type=css&sleep=1&expires=-1&last=0">
```

Both the image and stylesheet use the `expires=-1` option to get a response that has an `Expires` header in the past. This prevents the components from being cached so that you can run the test repeatedly and get the same experience each time (I also add a unique timestamp to each component's URL to further prevent caching). In order to reduce the variables in this test, I specify `last=0` to remove the `Last-Modified` header from the response. The image request has a two-second delay (`sleep=2`), while the stylesheet is delayed only one second (`sleep=1`). This ensures that any delay seen is not due to the stylesheet's response time, but instead to its blocking behavior (which is what the page is testing).

Being able to exaggerate the response times of components makes it possible to visualize their effects on page loading and response times. I've made the Perl code available so others can use it for their own testing (*http://stevesouders.com/hpws/sleep.txt*). Copy the code into an executable file named *sleep.cgi* and place it in an executable directory on your web server.

Blank White Screen

This section shows two web pages that differ in just one respect: whether the stylesheet is at the top or bottom of the page. What a difference it makes to the user experience!

CSS at the Bottom

The first example demonstrates the harm of putting stylesheets at the bottom of the HTML document.

CSS at the Bottom
http://stevesouders.com/hpws/css-bottom.php

Notice how putting stylesheets near the end of the document can delay page loading. This problem is harder to track down because it only happens in Internet Explorer and depends on how the page is loaded. After working with the page, you'll notice that it occasionally loads slowly. When this happens, the page is completely blank until all the content blasts onto the screen at once, as illustrated in Figure 5-1. Progressive rendering has been thwarted. This is a bad user experience because there is no visual feedback to reassure the user that her request is being handled correctly. Instead, the user is left to wonder whether anything is happening. That's the moment when a user abandons your web site and navigates to your competitor.

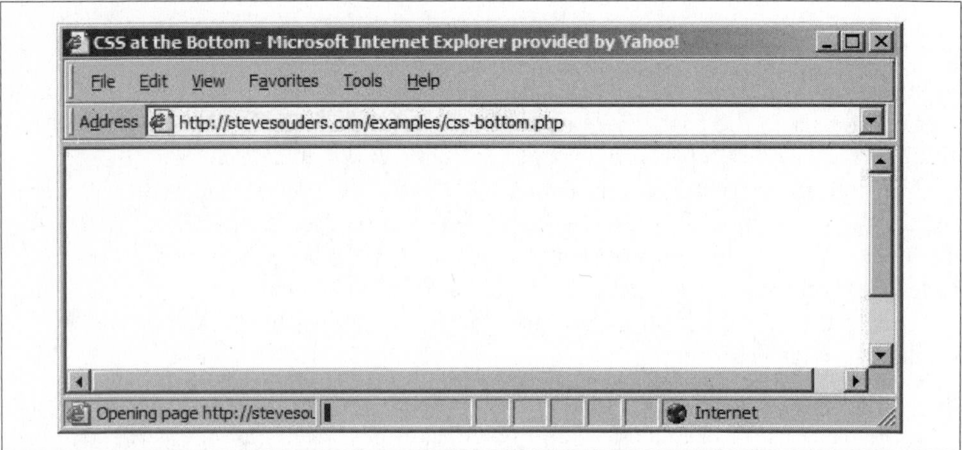

Figure 5-1. The blank white screen

Here are the cases where putting stylesheets at the bottom of the document causes the blank white screen problem to surface in Internet Explorer:

In a new window
: Clicking the "new window" link in the example page opens "CSS at the Bottom" in a new window. Users often open new windows when navigating across sites, such as when going from a search results page to the actual target page.

As a reload
: Clicking the Refresh button, a normal user behavior, is another way to trigger a blank white screen. Minimize and restore the window while the page is loading to see the blank white screen.

As a home page
: Setting the browser's default page to *http://stevesouders.com/hpws/css-bottom.php* and opening a new browser window causes the blank white screen. Rule 5 is important for any team that wants its web site to be used as a home page.

Solved! There's just one more complexity to point out.

There are two ways you can include a stylesheet in your document: the `LINK` tag and the `@import` rule. An example `LINK` tag looks like this:

```
<link rel="stylesheet" href="styles1.css">
```

This is an example of a `STYLE` block with an `@import` rule:

```
<style>
@import url("styles2.css");
</style>
```

A `STYLE` block can contain multiple `@import` rules, but `@import` rules must precede all other rules. I've seen cases where this is overlooked, and developers spend time trying to determine why the stylesheet isn't loaded from an `@import` rule. For this reason, I prefer using the `LINK` tag (one less thing to keep track of). Beyond the easier syntax, there are also performance benefits to using `LINK` instead of `@import`. The `@import` rule causes the blank white screen phenomenon, even if used in the document `HEAD`, as shown in the following example.

CSS at the Top Using @import
http://stevesouders.com/hpws/css-top-import.php

Using the `@import` rule causes an unexpected ordering in how the components are downloaded. Figure 5-2 shows the HTTP traffic for all three examples. Each page contains eight HTTP requests:

- One HTML page
- Six images
- One stylesheet

The components in *css-bottom.php* and *css-top.php* are downloaded in the order in which they appear in the document. However, even though *css-top-import.php* has the stylesheet at the top in the document `HEAD`, the stylesheet is downloaded *last* because it uses `@import`. As a result, it has the blank white screen problem, just like *css-bottom.php*.

Figure 5-2 also shows that the overall time for each page to load (including all of the page's components) is the same: about 7.3 seconds. It's surprising that the pages that feel slower, *css-bottom.php* and *css-top-import.php*, actually download all the page's necessary components faster. They finish downloading the HTML page and all six images in 6.3 seconds, while *css-top.php* takes 7.3 seconds to download the page's required components. It takes *css-top.php* one second longer because it downloads the stylesheet early on, even though it's not needed for rendering. This delays the download of the six images by about one second. Even though the necessary components take longer to download, *css-top.php* displays more quickly because it renders progressively.

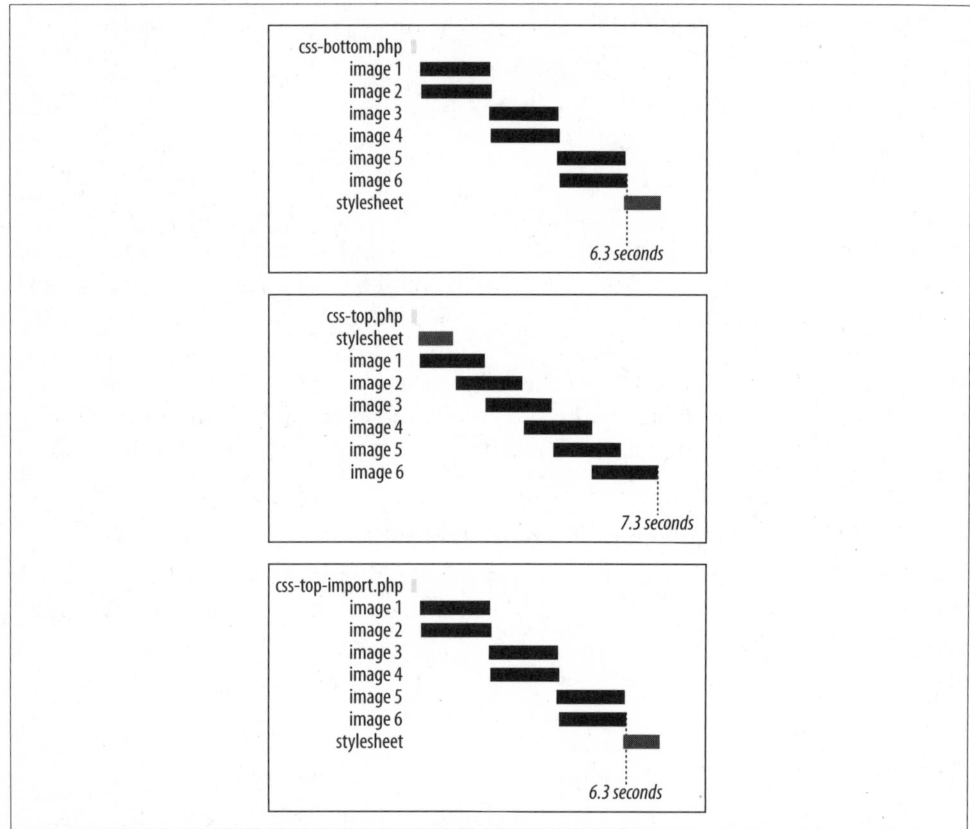

Figure 5-2. Loading components

Great! We know what to do: *put stylesheets in the document* HEAD *using the* LINK *tag*. But if you're like me you're asking yourself, "Why does the browser work this way?"

> If stylesheets are still loading, it is wasteful to construct the rendering tree, since you don't want to paint anything at all until all stylesheets have been loaded and parsed. Otherwise you'll run into a problem called FOUC (the flash of unstyled content problem), where you show content before it's ready.

The following example demonstrates this problem.

CSS Flash of Unstyled Content
http://stevesouders.com/hpws/css-fouc.php

In this example, the document uses one of the CSS rules from the stylesheet, but the stylesheet is (incorrectly) placed at the bottom. When the page loads progressively the text is displayed first, followed by the images as they arrive. Finally, when the stylesheet is successfully downloaded and parsed, the already-rendered text and images are redrawn using the new styles. This is the "flash of unstyled content" in action. It should be avoided.

The blank white screen is the browser's attempt to be forgiving to frontend engineers who mistakenly put their stylesheets too far down in the document. The blank white screen is the foil of the FOUC problem. The browser can delay rendering until all the stylesheets are downloaded, causing the blank white screen. By contrast, the browser can render progressively and risk flashing the user. Neither choice is ideal.

What's a Frontend Engineer to Do?

So how can you avoid both the blank white screen and the flash of unstyled content?

In the "CSS Flash of Unstyled Content" example, the flash doesn't always happen; it depends on your browser and how you load the page. Earlier in this chapter, I explained that the blank white screen happens in Internet Explorer only when the page is loaded in a new window, as a reload, or as a home page. In these cases, Internet Explorer chooses the blank white screen. However, if you click on a link, use a bookmark, or type a URL, Internet Explorer chooses the second alternative: risking FOUC.

* David Hyatt, "Surfin' Safari" blog, *http://weblogs.mozillazine.org/hyatt/archives/2004_05.html#005496*.

Firefox is more consistent—it always chooses the second alternative (FOUC). All the examples behave identically in Firefox: they render progressively. For the first three examples, Firefox's behavior works to the user's benefit because the stylesheet is not required for rendering the page, but in the "CSS Flash of Unstyled Content" example, the user is less fortunate. The user experiences the FOUC problem precisely because Firefox renders progressively.

When browsers behave differently, what's a frontend engineer to do?

You can find the answer in the HTML specification (*http://www.w3.org/TR/html4/struct/links.html#h-12.3*):

> Unlike A, [LINK] may only appear in the HEAD section of a document, although it may appear any number of times.

Browsers have a history of supporting practices that violate the HTML specification in order to make older, sloppier web pages work, but when it comes to handling the placement of stylesheets, Internet Explorer and Firefox are nudging the web development community to follow the specification. Pages that violate the specification (by putting the `LINK` outside of the `HEAD` section) still render, but risk a degraded user experience.

In their effort to improve one of the most visited pages on the Web, the Yahoo! portal team initially made it worse by moving the stylesheet to the bottom of the page. They found the optimal solution by following the HTML specification and leaving it at the top. Neither of the alternatives—the blank white screen or flash of unstyled content—are worth the risk. If you have a stylesheet that's not required to render the page, with some extra effort you can load it dynamically after the document loads, as described in the section "Post-Onload Download" in Chapter 8. Otherwise, whether your stylesheets are necessary to render the page or not, there's one rule to follow.

Put your stylesheets in the document `HEAD` using the `LINK` tag.

Chapter 5 described how stylesheets near the bottom of the page prohibit progressive rendering, and how moving them to the document HEAD eliminates the problem. Scripts (external JavaScript files) pose a similar problem, but the solution is just the opposite: it's better to move scripts from the top of the page to the bottom (when possible). This enables progressive rendering and achieves greater download parallelization. Let's first look at an example of these problems.

Problems with Scripts

The best way to demonstrate the issues with scripts is by using an example that has a script in the middle of the page.

Scripts in the Middle
    http://stevesouders.com/hpws/js-middle.php

This script is programmed to take 10 seconds to load, so it's easy to see the problem—the bottom half of the page takes about 10 seconds to appear (see the section "sleep.cgi" in Chapter 5 for an explanation of how components are configured to have specific load times). This occurs because the script blocks parallel downloading. We'll come back to this problem after a review of how browsers download in parallel.

The other problem with the example page has to do with progressive rendering. When using stylesheets, progressive rendering is blocked until all stylesheets have been downloaded. That's why it's best to move stylesheets to the document HEAD, so they are downloaded first and rendering isn't blocked. With scripts, progressive rendering is blocked for all content *below* the script. Moving scripts lower in the page means more content is rendered progressively.

Parallel Downloads

The biggest impact on response time is the number of components in the page. Each component generates an HTTP request when the cache is empty, and sometimes even when the cache is primed. Knowing that the browser performs HTTP requests in parallel, you may ask why the number of HTTP requests affects response time. Can't the browser download them all at once?

The explanation goes back to the HTTP/1.1 specification, which suggests that browsers download two components in parallel per hostname (*http://www.w3.org/Protocols/rfc2616/rfc2616-sec8.html#sec8.1.4*). Many web pages download all their components from a single hostname. Viewing these HTTP requests reveals a stair-step pattern, as shown in Figure 6-1.

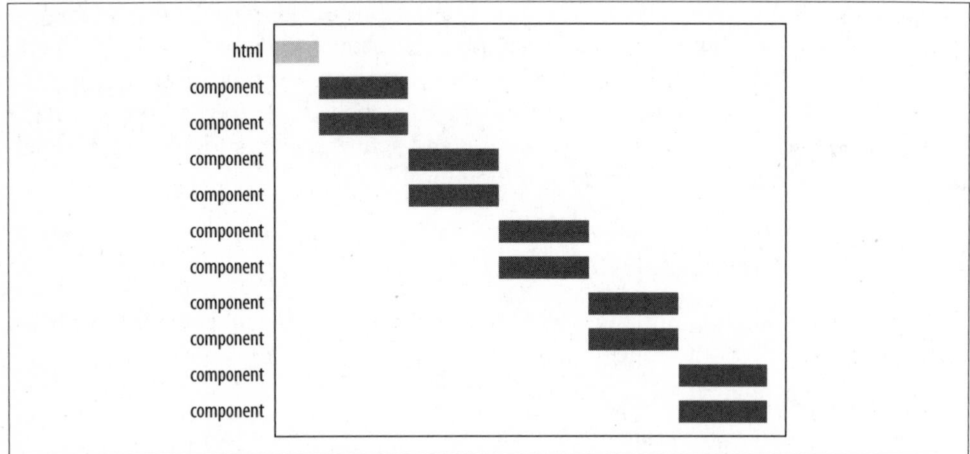

Figure 6-1. Downloading two components in parallel

If a web page evenly distributed its components across two hostnames, the overall response time would be about twice as fast. The HTTP requests would behave in the pattern shown in Figure 6-2, with four components downloaded in parallel (two per hostname). To give a visual cue as to how much faster this page loads, the horizontal width of the box is the same as in Figure 6-1.

Limiting parallel downloads to two per hostname is a guideline. By default, both Internet Explorer and Firefox follow the guideline, but users can override this default behavior. Internet Explorer stores the value in the Registry Editor.*

You can modify this default setting in Firefox by using the `network.http.max-persistent-connections-per-server` setting in the *about:config* page. It's interesting to note that for HTTP/1.0, Firefox's default is to download eight components in

* For more information about overriding this default, see Microsoft's web article "How to configure Internet Explorer to have more than two download sessions," *http://support.microsoft.com/?kbid=282402*.

Figure 6-2. Downloading four components in parallel

parallel per hostname. Figure 6-3 shows that Firefox's settings for HTTP/1.0 result in the fastest response time for this hypothetical page. It's even faster than that shown in Figure 6-2, even though only one hostname is used.

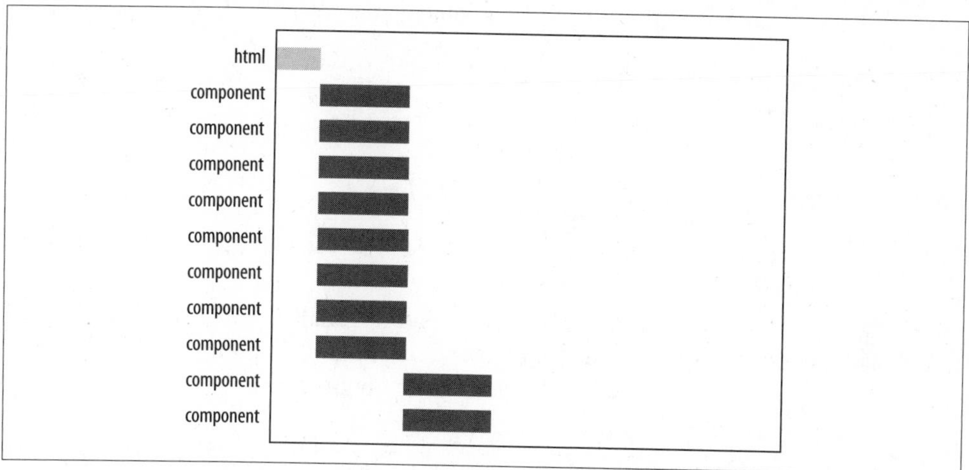

Figure 6-3. Downloading eight components in parallel (default for Firefox HTTP/1.0)

Most web sites today use HTTP/1.1, but the idea of increasing parallel downloads beyond two per hostname is intriguing. Instead of relying on users to modify their browser settings, frontend engineers could simply use CNAMEs (DNS aliases) to split their components across multiple hostnames. Maximizing parallel downloads doesn't come without a cost. Depending on your bandwidth and CPU speed, too many parallel downloads can degrade performance. Research at Yahoo! shows that splitting components across two hostnames leads to better performance than using 1, 4, or 10 hostnames.*

Scripts Block Downloads

The benefits of downloading components in parallel are clear. However, parallel downloading is actually *disabled* while a script is downloading—the browser won't start any other downloads, even on different hostnames. One reason for this behavior is that the script may use `document.write` to alter the page content, so the browser waits to make sure the page is laid out appropriately.

Another reason that the browser blocks parallel downloads when scripts are being loaded is to guarantee that the scripts are executed in the proper order. If multiple scripts were downloaded in parallel, there's no guarantee the responses would arrive in the order specified. For example, if the last script was smaller than scripts that appear earlier on the page, it might return first. If there were dependencies between the scripts, executing them out of order would result in JavaScript errors. The following example demonstrates how scripts block parallel downloads.

Scripts Block Downloads
http://stevesouders.com/hpws/js-blocking.php

This page contains the following components in this order:

1. An image from host1
2. An image from host2
3. A script from host1 that takes 10 seconds to load
4. An image from host1
5. An image from host2

Given the description of how browsers download in parallel, you would expect that the two images from host2 would be downloaded in parallel, along with the first two components from host1. Figure 6-4 shows what really happens.

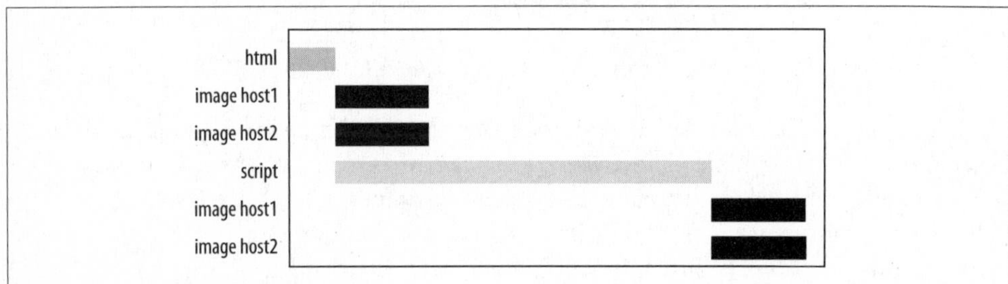

Figure 6-4. Scripts block downloads

* Tenni Theurer, "Performance Research, Part 4: Maximizing Parallel Downloads in the Carpool Lane," *http://yuiblog.com/blog/2007/04/11/performance-research-part-4/*.

Worst Case: Scripts at the Top

At this point, the effects that scripts can have on web pages are clear:

- Content below the script is blocked from rendering.
- Components below the script are blocked from being downloaded.

If scripts are put at the top of the page, as they usually are, *everything* in the page is below the script, and the entire page is blocked from rendering and downloading until the script is loaded. Try out the following example.

Scripts at the Top
http://stevesouders.com/hpws/js-top.php

Because this entire page is blocked from rendering, it results in the blank white screen phenomenon described in Chapter 5. Progressive rendering is critical for a good user experience, but slow scripts delay the feedback users crave. Also, the reduction of parallelized downloads delays how quickly images are displayed in the page. Figure 6-5 shows how the components in the page are downloaded later than desired.

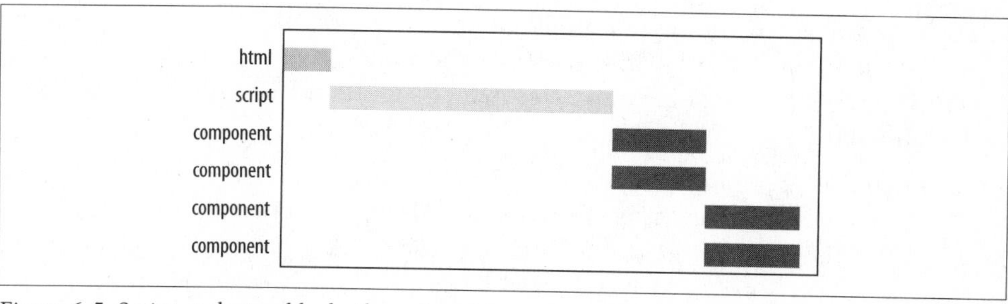

Figure 6-5. Script at the top blocks the entire page

Best Case: Scripts at the Bottom

The best place to put scripts is at the bottom of the page. The page contents aren't blocked from rendering, and the viewable components in the page are downloaded as early as possible. Figure 6-6 shows how the long request for the script has less of an effect on the page when it is placed at the bottom. You can see this by visiting the following example.

Scripts at the Bottom
http://stevesouders.com/hpws/js-bottom.php

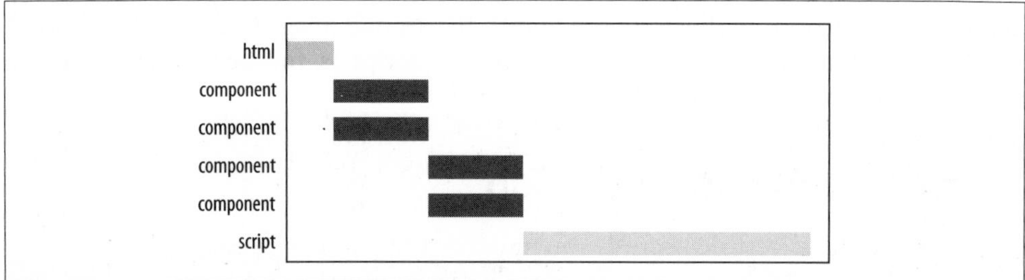

Figure 6-6. Scripts at the bottom have the least impact

The benefit is really highlighted by viewing the pages with scripts at the top versus scripts at the bottom side-by-side. You can see this in the following example.

Scripts Top vs. Bottom
http://stevesouders.com/hpws/move-scripts.php

Putting It in Perspective

These examples use a script that takes 10 seconds to download. Hopefully, the delay isn't as long for any scripts you use, but it is possible for a script to take longer than expected and for the user's bandwidth to affect the response time of a script. The effect that scripts have on your pages might be less than shown here, but it could still be noticeable. Having multiple scripts in your page compounds the problem.

In some situations, it's not easy to move scripts to the bottom. If, for example, the script uses `document.write` to insert part of the page's content, it can't be moved lower in the page. There might also be scoping issues. In many cases, there are ways to work around these situations.

An alternative suggestion that comes up often is to use *deferred* scripts. The `DEFER` attribute indicates that the script does not contain `document.write`, and is a clue to browsers that they can continue rendering. You can see this in the following example.

Deferred Scripts
http://stevesouders.com/hpws/js-defer.php

Unfortunately, in Firefox, even deferred scripts block rendering and parallel downloads. In Internet Explorer, components lower in the page are downloaded slightly later. If a script can be deferred, it can also be moved to the bottom of the page. That's the best thing to do to speed up your web pages.

Move scripts to the bottom of the page.

CSS expressions are a powerful (and dangerous) way to set CSS properties dynamically. They're supported in Internet Explorer version 5 and later. Let's start with a conventional CSS rule for setting the background color:

```
background-color: #B8D4FF;
```

For a more dynamic page, the background color could be set to alternate every hour using CSS expressions.

```
background-color: expression( (new Date()).getHours()%2 ? "#B8D4FF" : "#F08A00" );
```

As shown here, the `expression` method accepts a JavaScript expression. The CSS property is set to the result of evaluating the JavaScript expression.

The `expression` method is simply ignored by other browsers, so it is a useful tool for setting properties in Internet Explorer to create a consistent experience across browsers. For example, Internet Explorer does not support the `min-width` property. CSS expressions are one way to solve this problem. The following example ensures that a page width is always at least 600 pixels, using an expression that Internet Explorer respects and a static setting honored by other browsers:

```
width: expression( document.body.clientWidth < 600 ? "600px" : "auto" );
min-width: 600px;
```

Most browsers ignore the `width` property here because they don't support CSS expressions and instead use the `min-width` property. Internet Explorer ignores the `min-width` property and instead sets the `width` property dynamically based on the width of the document. CSS expressions are re-evaluated when the page changes, such as when it is resized. This ensures that as the user resizes his browser, the width is adjusted appropriately. The frequency with which CSS expressions are evaluated is what makes them work, but it is also what makes CSS expressions bad for performance.

Updating Expressions

The problem with expressions is that they are evaluated more frequently than most people expect. Not only are they evaluated whenever the page is rendered and resized, but also when the page is scrolled and even when the user moves the mouse over the page. Adding a counter to the CSS expression allows us to keep track of when and how often a CSS expression is evaluated.

Expression Counter
    http://stevesouders.com/hpws/expression-counter.php

The CSS expression counter example has the following CSS rule:

```
P {
  width: expression( setCntr( ), document.body.clientWidth<600 ? "600px" : "auto" );
  min-width: 600px;
  border: 1px solid;
}
```

The `setCntr( )` function increments a global variable and writes the value in the text field in the page. There are 10 paragraphs in the page. Loading the page executes the CSS expression 40 times. Subsequent to that, the CSS expression is evaluated 10 times for various events including resize, scrolling, and mouse movements. Moving the mouse around the page can easily generate more than 10,000 evaluations. The danger of CSS expressions is evident in this example. Worst of all, clicking in the text input field locks up Internet Explorer, and you have to kill the process.

Working Around the Problem

Most CSS experts are familiar with CSS expressions and how to avoid the pitfalls highlighted by the previous example. Two techniques for avoiding problems created by CSS expressions are creating one-time expressions and using event handlers instead of CSS expressions.

One-Time Expressions

If the CSS expression has to be evaluated only once, it can overwrite itself as part of its execution. The background style defined at the beginning of this chapter is a good candidate for this approach:

```
<style>
P {
    background-color: expression( altBgcolor(this) );
}
</style>

<script type="text/javascript">
```

times, much better than the tens of thousands in the previous example.

One-Time Expressions
: *http://stevesouders.com/hpws/onetime-expressions.php*

Event Handlers

In most situations where I've seen CSS expressions used, it was possible to find an alternative that didn't require them. CSS expressions benefit from being automatically tied to events in the browser, but that's also their downfall. Instead of using CSS expressions, the frontend engineer can do the "heavy lifting" by tying the desired dynamic behavior to the appropriate event using event handlers. This avoids the evaluation of the expression during unrelated events. The event handler example demonstrates a fix to the `min-width` problem by setting the style's `width` property with the `onresize` event, avoiding tens of thousands of unnecessary evaluations during mouse movements, scrolling, etc.

Event Handler
: *http://stevesouders.com/hpws/event-handler.php*

This example uses the `setMinWidth()` function to resize all paragraph elements when the browser is resized:

```
function setMinWidth( ) {
    setCntr( );
    var aElements = document.getElementsByTagName("p");
    for ( var i = 0; i < aElements.length; i++ ) {
        aElements[i].runtimeStyle.width = ( document.body.clientWidth<600 ?
"600px" : "auto" );
     }
}

if ( -1 != navigator.userAgent.indexOf("MSIE") ) {
    window.onresize = setMinWidth;
}
```

This sets the width dynamically when the browser is resized, but it does not size the paragraph appropriately when it is first rendered. Therefore, the page also uses the approach shown in the "One-Time Expressions" section to set the initial width using CSS expressions, while overwriting the CSS expression after its first evaluation.

Conclusion

This is one of the few rules that addresses performance of the page *after* it has been loaded, which is generally when CSS expressions cause problems. However, in some cases, CSS expressions can affect the load time of a page, too. One property at Yahoo! had a CSS expression that caused a 20-second delay during the initial rendering of the page. This result was unexpected and took a while to diagnose. Similarly, who would have thought the CSS expression used in the "Expression Counter" example would cause Internet Explorer to lock up if the user clicked in a text field? A full discussion of complicated CSS incompatibilities, such as `min-width` and `position: fixed`, is beyond the scope of this book, and that's the point—using CSS expressions without a deep understanding of the underlying implications is dangerous.

> Avoid CSS expressions.

Many of the performance rules in this book deal with how external components are managed, such as serving them via a CDN (Rule 2), making sure they have a far future `Expires` header (Rule 3), and compressing their contents (Rule 4). However, before these considerations arise, you should ask a more basic question: should JavaScript and CSS be contained in external files or inlined in the page itself? As we'll see, using external files is generally better.

Inline vs. External

Let's first start with the tradeoffs in placing JavaScript and CSS inline versus using external files.

In Raw Terms, Inline Is Faster

I have generated two examples that demonstrate how inlining JavaScript and CSS results in faster response times than making them external files.

Inlined JS and CSS
: *http://stevesouders.com/hpws/inlined.php*

External JS and CSS
: *http://stevesouders.com/hpws/external.php*

The inline example involves one HTML document that is 87K, with all of the JavaScript and CSS in the page itself. The external example contains an HTML document (7K), one stylesheet (59K), and three scripts (1K, 11K, and 9K) for a total of 87K. Although the total amount of data downloaded is the same, the inline example is 30–50% faster than the external example. This is primarily because the external example suffers from the overhead of multiple HTTP requests (see Chapter 1 about the importance of minimizing HTTP requests). The external example even benefits from the stylesheet and scripts being downloaded in parallel, but the difference of one HTTP request compared to five is what makes the inline example faster.

Despite these results, using external files in the real world generally produces faster pages. This is due to a benefit of external files that is not captured by these examples: the opportunity for the JavaScript and CSS files to be cached by the browser. HTML documents, at least those that contain dynamic content, are typically not configured to be cached. When this is the case (when the HTML documents are not cached), the inline JavaScript and CSS is downloaded every time the HTML document is requested. On the other hand, if the JavaScript and CSS are in external files cached by the browser, the size of the HTML document is reduced without increasing the number of HTTP requests.

The key factor, then, is the frequency with which external JavaScript and CSS components are cached relative to the number of HTML documents requested. This factor, although difficult to quantify, can be gauged using the following metrics.

Page Views

The fewer page views per user, the stronger the argument for inlining JavaScript and CSS. Imagine that a typical user visits your site once per month. Between visits, it's likely that any external JavaScript and CSS files have been purged from the browser's cache, even if the components have a far future `Expires` header (see Chapter 3 for more information about using a far future `Expires` header).

On the other hand, if a typical user has many page views, the browser is more likely to have external components (with a far future `Expires` header) in its cache. The benefit of serving JavaScript and CSS using external files grows along with the number of page views per user per month or page views per user per session.

Empty Cache vs. Primed Cache

Knowing the potential for users to cache external components is critical to comparing inlining versus external files. We measured this at Yahoo! and found that the number of unique users coming in at least once a day with a primed cache ranges from 40–60% depending on the Yahoo! property.* The same study revealed that the number of page views with a primed cache is 75–85%. Note that the first statistic measures "unique users" while the second measures "page views." The percentage of page views with a primed cache is higher than the percentage of unique users with a primed cache because many users perform multiple page views per session. Users may show up once during the day with an empty cache, but make several subsequent page views with a primed cache. See more information about this research in Chapter 3.

* Tenni Theurer, "Performance Research, Part 2: Browser Cache Usage – Exposed!", *http://yuiblog.com/blog/2007/01/04/performance-research-part-2/*.

If every page on your site uses the same JavaScript and CSS, using external files will result in a high reuse rate for these components. Using external files becomes more advantageous in this situation because the JavaScript and CSS components are already in the browser's cache while users navigate across pages.

The opposite end of the spectrum is also easy to comprehend—if no two pages share the same JavaScript and CSS, the reuse rate will be low. The difficulty is that most web sites aren't this black and white. This raises a separate but related issue: where do you draw the boundaries when packaging JavaScript and CSS into external files?

The debate starts with the premise that fewer files are better (see Chapter 1 for a more detailed analysis). In a typical situation, the reuse of JavaScript and CSS across pages is neither 100% overlapping nor 100% disjointed. In this middle-case scenario, one extreme is to make a separate set of external files for each page. The downside of this approach is that every page subjects the user to another set of external components and resulting HTTP requests that slow down response times. This alternative makes the most sense on sites where a typical user visits only one page and there is little cross-page traffic.

The other extreme is to create a single file that is the union of all the JavaScript, and create another single file for all of the CSS. This has the benefit of subjecting the user to only one HTTP request, but it increases the amount of data downloaded on a user's first page view. In this case, users will be downloading more JavaScript and CSS than is necessary for the page currently being viewed. Also, this single file must be updated whenever any of the individual scripts or stylesheets changes, invalidating the version currently cached by all users. This alternative makes the most sense on sites with a high number of sessions per user per month, where the typical session includes visits to multiple different pages.

If your site doesn't fit nicely into one of these extremes, the best answer is a compromise. Categorize your pages into a handful of page types and then create a single script and stylesheet for each one. These are not as easy to maintain as a single file, but are typically much easier to maintain than different scripts and stylesheets for each page, and they result in less superfluous JavaScript and CSS being downloaded for any given page.

Ultimately, your decision about the boundaries for JavaScript and CSS external files affects the degree of component reuse. If you can find a balance that results in a high reuse rate, the argument is stronger for deploying your JavaScript and CSS as external files. If the reuse rate is low, inlining might make more sense.

Typical Results in the Field

In analyzing the tradeoffs between inlining versus using external files, the key is the frequency with which external JavaScript and CSS components are cached relative to the number of HTML documents requested. In the previous section, I described three metrics (page views, empty cache vs. primed cache, and component reuse) that can help you determine the best option. The right answer for any specific web site depends on these metrics.

Many web sites fall in the middle of these metrics. They get 5–15 page views per user per month, with 2–5 page views per user per session. Empty cache visits are in the same range as Yahoo!: 40–60% of unique users per day have a primed cache, and 75–85% of page views per day are performed with a primed cache. There's a fair amount of JavaScript and CSS reuse across pages, resulting in a handful of files that cover every major page type.

For sites that have these metrics, the best solution is generally to deploy the JavaScript and CSS as external files. This is demonstrated by the example where the external components can be cached by the browser. Loading this page repeatedly and comparing the results to those of the first example, "Inlined JS and CSS," shows that using external files with a far future `Expires` header is the fastest approach.

Cacheable External JS and CSS
: *http://stevesouders.com/hpws/external-cacheable.php*

Home Pages

The only exception I've seen where inlining is preferable is with home pages. A home page is the URL chosen as the browser's default page, such as Yahoo! home page (*http://www.yahoo.com*) and My Yahoo! (*http://my.yahoo.com*). Let's look at the three metrics from the perspective of home pages:

Page views
: Home pages have a high number of page views per month. By definition, whenever the browser is opened, the home page is visited. However, there is often only one page view per session.

Empty cache vs. primed cache
: The primed cache percentage might be lower than other sites. For security reasons, many users elect to clear the cache every time they close the browser. The next time they open the browser it generates an empty cache page view of the home page.

the last thing they want is a slow home page. For the company's home page campaign to succeed, the page must be fast.

There's no single answer that applies to all home pages. The factors highlighted here must be evaluated for the home page in question. If inlining is the right answer, you'll find helpful information in the next section, which describes two techniques that have the benefit of inlining while taking advantage of external files (when possible).

The Best of Both Worlds

Even if all the factors point to inlining, it still feels inefficient to add all that JavaScript and CSS to the page and not take advantage of the browser's cache. Two techniques are described here that allow you to gain the benefits of inlining, as well as caching external files.

Post-Onload Download

Some home pages, like Yahoo! home page and My Yahoo!, typically have only one page view per session. However, that's not the case for all home pages. Yahoo! Mail is a good example of a home page that often leads to secondary page views (pages that are accessed after the initial page, such as those for viewing or composing email messages).

For home pages that are the first of many page views, we want to inline the JavaScript and CSS for the home page, but leverage external files for all secondary page views. This is accomplished by dynamically downloading the external components in the home page after it has completely loaded (via the `onload` event). This places the external files in the browser's cache in anticipation of the user continuing on to other pages.

Post-Onload Download
: *http://stevesouders.com/hpws/post-onload.php*

The post-onload download JavaScript code associates the `doOnload` function with the document's `onload` event. After a one-second delay (to make sure the page is completely rendered), the appropriate JavaScript and CSS files are downloaded. This is done by creating the appropriate DOM elements (`script` and `link`, respectively) and assigning the specific URL:

```
<script type="text/javascript">
function doOnload() {
    setTimeout("downloadComponents()", 1000);
}

window.onload = doOnload;

// Download external components dynamically using JavaScript.
function downloadComponents() {
    downloadJS("http://stevesouders.com/hpws/testsma.js");
    downloadCSS("http://stevesouders.com/hpws/testsm.css");
}

// Download a script dynamically.
function downloadJS(url) {
    var elem = document.createElement("script");
    elem.src = url;
    document.body.appendChild(elem);
}

// Download a stylesheet dynamically.
function downloadCSS(url) {
    var elem = document.createElement("link");
    elem.rel = "stylesheet";
    elem.type = "text/css";
    elem.href = url;
    document.body.appendChild(elem);
}
</script>
```

In these pages, the JavaScript and CSS are loaded twice into the page (inline then external). To work, your code has to deal with *double definition*. Scripts, for example, can *define* but can't *execute* any functions (at least none that the user notices). CSS that uses relative metrics (percentages or `em`) may be problematic if applied twice. Inserting these components into an invisible IFrame is a more advanced approach that avoids these problems.

Dynamic Inlining

If a home page server knew whether a component was in the browser's cache, it could make the optimal decision about whether to inline or use external files. Although there is no way for a server to see what's in the browser's cache, cookies can be used as an indicator. By returning a session-based cookie with the component, the home page server can make a decision about inlining based on the absence or presence of the cookie. If the cookie is absent, the JavaScript or CSS is inlined. If the cookie is present, it's likely the external component is in the browser's cache and external files are used. The "Dynamic Inlining" example demonstrates this technique.

page has loaded. The next time the page is visited, the server sees the cookie and generates a page that uses external files.

The PHP code that handles the dynamic behavior is shown below:

```
<?php
if ( $_COOKIE["CA"] ) {
    // If the cookie is present, it's likely the component is cached.
    // Use external files since they'll just be read from disk.
    echo <<<OUTPUT
<link rel="stylesheet" href="testsm.css" type="text/css">
<script src="testsma.js" type="text/javascript"></script>
OUTPUT;
}
else {
    // If the cookie is NOT present, it's likely the component is NOT cached.
    // Inline all the components and trigger a post-onload download of the files.
    echo "<style>\n" . file_get_contents("testsm.css") . "</style>\n";
    echo "<script type=\"text/javascript\">\n" . file_get_contents("testsma.js") .
"</script>\n";
    // Output the Post-Onload Download JavaScript code here.
    echo <<<ONLOAD
<script type="text/javascript">
function doOnload( ) {
    setTimeout("downloadComponents( )", 1000);
}

window.onload = doOnload;

// Download external components dynamically using JavaScript.
function downloadComponents( ) {
    document.cookie = "CA=1";
[snip...]
ONLOAD;
}
?>
```

I didn't show all of the post-onload download JavaScript code (as indicated by "[snip...]") since that was included earlier in the "Post-Onload Download" section. However, I did show just enough to illustrate how the `CA` cookie is set in the `downloadComponents` function. This is the only change, but it's key to leveraging the cache on subsequent page views.

The beauty of this approach is how forgiving it is. If there's a mismatch between the state of the cookie and the state of the cache, the page still works. It's not as optimized as it could be. The session-based cookie technique errs on the side of inlining even though the components are in the browser's cache—if the user reopens the browser, the session-based cookie is absent but the components may still be cached. Changing the cookie from session-based to short-lived (hours or days) addresses this issue, but moves toward erring on the side of using external files when they're not truly in the browser's cache. Either way, the page still works, and across all users there is an improvement in response times by more intelligently choosing between inlining versus using external files.

> Put your JavaScript and CSS in external files.

The Internet is based on finding servers through IP addresses. Because IP addresses are hard to remember, URLs typically contain hostnames instead, but the IP address is still necessary for the browser to make its request. That's the role of the Domain Name System (DNS). DNS maps hostnames to IP addresses, just as phonebooks map people's names to their phone numbers. When you type *www.yahoo.com* into your browser, a DNS resolver is contacted by the browser and returns that server's IP address.

This explanation highlights another benefit of DNS—a layer of indirection between URLs and the actual servers that host them. If a server is replaced with one that has a different IP address, DNS allows users to use the same hostname to connect to the new server. Or, as is the case with *www.yahoo.com*, multiple IP addresses can be associated with a hostname, providing a high degree of redundancy for a web site.

However, DNS has a cost. It typically takes 20–120 milliseconds for the browser to look up the IP address for a given hostname. The browser can't download anything from this hostname until the DNS lookup is completed. The response time depends on the DNS resolver (typically provided by your ISP), the load of requests on it, your proximity to it, and your bandwidth speed. After reviewing how DNS works from the browser's perspective, I'll describe what you can do to reduce the amount of time your pages spend doing DNS lookups.

DNS Caching and TTLs

DNS lookups are cached for better performance. This caching can occur on a special caching server maintained by the user's ISP or local area network, but here we'll explore DNS caching on the individual user's computer. As shown in Figure 9-1, after a user requests a hostname, the DNS information remains in the operating system's DNS cache (the "DNS Client service" on Microsoft Windows), and further requests for that hostname don't require more DNS lookups, at least not for a while.

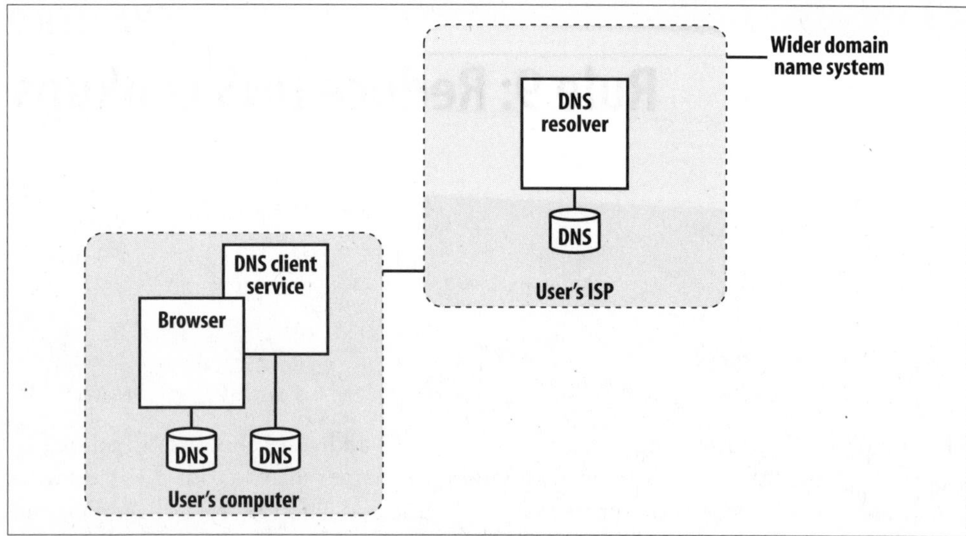

Figure 9-1. DNS caching from the browser's perspective

Simple enough? Hold on a minute—most browsers have their own caches, separate from the operating system's cache. As long as the browser keeps a DNS record in its own cache, it doesn't bother the operating system with a request for the record. Only after the browser's cache discards the record does it ask the operating system for the address—and then the operating system either satisfies the request out of its cache or sends a request to a remote server, which is where potential slowdowns occur.

To make things yet more complicated, designers realize that IP addresses change and that caches consume memory. Therefore, the DNS records have to be periodically flushed from the cache, and several different configuration settings determine how often they are discarded.

Factors Affecting DNS Caching

First, the server has a say in how long records should be cached. The DNS record returned from a lookup contains a time-to-live (TTL) value. This tells the client how long the record can be cached.

Although operating system caches respect the TTL, browsers often ignore it and set their own time limits. Furthermore, the Keep-Alive feature of the HTTP protocol, discussed in Chapter B, can override both the TTL and the browser's time limit. In other words, as long as the browser and the web server are happily communicating and keeping their TCP connection open, there's no reason for a DNS lookup.

Browsers put a limit on the number of DNS records cached, regardless of the time the records have been in the cache. If the user visits many different sites with different

The maximum TTL values sent to clients for 10 top U.S. web sites range from one minute to one hour, as shown in Table 9-1.

Table 9-1. TTL values

Domain	TTL
http://www.amazon.com	1 minute
http://www.aol.com	1 minute
http://www.cnn.com	10 minutes
http://www.ebay.com	1 hour
http://www.google.com	5 minutes
http://www.msn.com	5 minutes
http://www.myspace.com	1 hour
http://www.wikipedia.org	1 hour
http://www.yahoo.com	1 minute
http://www.youtube.com	5 minutes

Why do these values vary so much? It's probably a mixture of intentional and historical factors. An interesting RFC* provides more details about the format of DNS records and common mistakes made when configuring them. Its first suggestion is to avoid making the TTL values too short, with a recommended value of one day!

These top web sites, given their large numbers of users, strive to have DNS resolvers quickly failover when a server, virtual IP address (VIP), or co-location goes offline. That's the reason for Yahoo!'s short TTL. MySpace, on the other hand, is located in one co-location facility. Failover is less critical given their current network topology, so a longer TTL is chosen because it reduces the number of DNS lookups, which in turn reduces the load on their name servers.

Making DNS configuration recommendations is beyond the scope of this book. What is most relevant, however, is how DNS caching affects the performance of web pages. Let's view DNS caching from the browser's perspective to determine how many DNS lookups your web pages cause.

* "Common DNS Data File Configuration Errors," *http://tools.ietf.org/html/rfc1537*.

The average TTL value received by the client for a DNS record is half of the maximum TTL value. That's because the DNS resolver itself has a TTL associated with its DNS record. When the browser does a DNS lookup, the DNS resolver returns the amount of time remaining in the TTL for its record. If the maximum TTL is 5 minutes, the TTL returned by the DNS resolver ranges from 1 to 300 seconds, with an average value of 150 seconds. The TTL received for a given hostname varies each time the DNS lookup is performed.

The Browser's Perspective

As discussed earlier in the "Factors Affecting DNS Caching" section, a lot of independent variables determine whether a particular browser request for a hostname makes a remote DNS request. There is a DNS specification (*http://tools.ietf.org/html/rfc1034*), but it gives clients flexibility in how the DNS cache works. I'll focus on Internet Explorer and Firefox on Microsoft Windows, since they are the most popular platforms.

The DNS cache on Microsoft Windows is managed by the DNS Client service. You can view and flush the DNS Client service using the `ipconfig` command:

```
ipconfig /displaydns
ipconfig /flushdns
```

Rebooting also clears the DNS Client service cache. In addition to the DNS Client service, Internet Explorer and Firefox browsers have their own DNS caches. Restarting the browser clears the browser cache, but not the DNS Client service cache.

Internet Explorer

Internet Explorer's DNS cache is controlled by three registry settings: `DnsCacheTimeout`, `KeepAliveTimeout`, and `ServerInfoTimeOut`, which can be created in the following registry key:

```
HKEY_CURRENT_USER\Software\Microsoft\Windows\CurrentVersion\InternetSettings\
```

There are two Microsoft Support articles describing how these settings affect the DNS cache.* These articles report the following default values for these settings:

- `DnsCacheTimeout`: 30 minutes
- `KeepAliveTimeout`: 1 minute
- `ServerInfoTimeOut`: 2 minutes

* "How Internet Explorer uses the cache for DNS host entries," *http://support.microsoft.com/default.aspx?scid=KB;en-us;263558*.

"How to change the default keep-alive time-out value in Internet Explorer," *http://support.microsoft.com/kb/813827*.

until it has been idle for one minute. Because the connection persists, a DNS lookup is not required (the benefits of Keep-Alive are discussed in Chapter B). This is an additional benefit—Keep-Alive avoids repeated DNS lookups by reusing the existing connection.

The `ServerInfoTimeOut` value of two minutes says that even without Keep-Alive, if a hostname is reused every two minutes without failure, a DNS lookup is not required. In tests using Internet Explorer, if a hostname is reused at least every two minutes, no DNS lookups are done even beyond 30 minutes (assuming there are no failures reaching that IP address).

This is important information for network operations centers when trying to divert traffic by making DNS changes. If the IP addresses that the traffic is being diverted from are left running, it will take at least 30 minutes for Internet Explorer users with the old DNS record to get the DNS update. Users actively hitting the site (at least once every two minutes) will keep going to the old IP address and never get the DNS update until a failure occurs.

Firefox

Firefox is quite a bit simpler to figure out. It has the following configuration settings:

- `network.dnsCacheExpiration`: 1 minute
- `network.dnsCacheEntries`: 20
- `network.http.keep-alive.timeout`: 5 minutes

DNS records are cached for one minute beyond their TTLs. Because of this low value, setting your TTLs low (less than an hour) is likely to increase the number of DNS lookups required by your pages in Firefox.

Surprisingly, only 20 records are cached in Firefox by default. This means that users who visit a lot of sites in different domains will be slowed down by DNS lookups more than Internet Explorer users with the same behavior.

Firefox's Keep-Alive timeout is higher than Internet Explorer's: five minutes versus one minute. Making sure your servers support Keep-Alive reduces the number of DNS lookups required by users navigating your web site.

Fasterfox (*http://fasterfox.mozdev.org*) is a well-known Firefox add-on for measuring and improving Firefox performance. As a point of comparison, Fasterfox changes these DNS settings to have the following values:

- `network.dnsCacheExpiration`: 1 hour
- `network.dnsCacheEntries`: 512
- `network.http.keep-alive.timeout`: 30 seconds

Reducing DNS Lookups

When the client's DNS cache is empty (for both the browser and the operating system), the number of DNS lookups is equal to the number of unique hostnames in the web page. This includes the hostnames used in the page's URL, images, script files, stylesheets, Flash objects, etc. Reducing the number of unique hostnames reduces the number of DNS lookups. Google (*http://www.google.com*) is the preeminent example of this, with only one DNS lookup necessary for the page.

Reducing the number of unique hostnames has the potential to reduce the amount of parallel downloading that takes place in the page. Avoiding DNS lookups cuts response times, but reducing parallel downloads may increase response times. As described in Chapter 6 in the section "Parallel Downloads," some amount of parallelization is good, even if it increases the number of hostnames. In the case of Google.com, there are only two components in the page. Because components are downloaded two per hostname in parallel, using one hostname minimizes the number of possible DNS lookups while maximizing parallel downloads.

Most pages today have a dozen or more components—not nearly as lean as Google. My guideline is to split these components across at least two but no more than four hostnames. This results in a good compromise between reducing DNS lookups and allowing a high degree of parallel downloads.

The advantage of using Keep-Alive, described in Chapter B, is that it reuses an existing connection, thereby improving response times by avoiding TCP/IP overhead. As described here, making sure your servers support Keep-Alive also reduces DNS lookups, especially for Firefox users.

> Reduce DNS lookups by using Keep-Alive and fewer domains.

JavaScript, being an interpreted language, is great for building web pages. Interpreted languages excel when developing user interfaces where rapid prototyping is the norm. Without a compilation step, though, the responsibility falls on the frontend engineer to optimize the JavaScript before final deployment. One aspect of this, gzipping, is discussed in Chapter 4. In this chapter, I describe another step that should be integrated into the JavaScript deployment process: minification.

Minification

Minification is the practice of removing unnecessary characters from code to reduce its size, thereby improving load times. When code is minified, all comments are removed, as well as unneeded whitespace characters (space, newline, and tab). In the case of JavaScript, this improves response time performance because the size of the downloaded file is reduced.

Table 10-1 shows how many of the 10 top U.S. web sites practice JavaScript minification—4 out of 10 minify their JavaScript code.

Table 10-1. Minification practices across 10 top web sites

Web site	External scripts minified?
http://www.amazon.com/	No
http://www.aol.com/	No
http://www.cnn.com/	No
http://www.ebay.com/	Yes
http://froogle.google.com/	Yes
http://www.msn.com/	Yes
http://www.myspace.com/	No
http://www.wikipedia.org/	No
http://www.yahoo.com/	Yes
http://www.youtube.com/	No

Let's look at what the others could have saved if they had minified. But first, I need to mention a more aggressive alternative to minification: obfuscation.

Obfuscation

Obfuscation is an alternative optimization that can be applied to source code. Like minification, it removes comments and whitespace, but it also munges the code. As part of munging, function and variable names are converted into smaller strings making the code more compact, as well as harder to read. This is typically done to make it more difficult to reverse-engineer the code, but munging can help performance because it reduces the code size beyond what is achieved by minification.

Assuming that thwarting reverse-engineering is not your objective, the question arises about whether to minify or obfuscate. Minification is a safe, fairly straightforward process. Obfuscation, on the other hand, is more complex. There are three main drawbacks to obfuscating your JavaScript code:

Bugs
: Because obfuscation is more complex, there's a higher probability of introducing errors into the code as a result of the obfuscation process itself.

Maintenance
: Since obfuscators change JavaScript symbols, any symbols that should not be changed (for example, API functions) have to be tagged so that the obfuscator leaves them unaltered.

Debugging
: Obfuscated code is more difficult to read. This makes debugging problems in your production environment more difficult.

Although I've never seen problems introduced from minification, I have seen bugs caused by obfuscation. Given the large amount of JavaScript maintained at Yahoo!, my guidelines recommend minification over obfuscation. The ultimate decision has to consider the additional size reductions achieved from obfuscation. In the next section, we'll do some real minifying and obfuscating.

The Savings

The most popular tool for minifying JavaScript code is JSMin (*http://crockford.com/javascript/jsmin*), developed by Douglas Crockford, a fellow Yahoo!. The JSMin source code is available in C, C#, Java, JavaScript, Perl, PHP, Python, and Ruby. The tool of choice is less clear in the area of JavaScript obfuscation. Dojo Compressor (renamed ShrinkSafe and moved to *http://dojotoolkit.org/docs/shrinksafe*) is the one I've seen used the most. For the purposes of our comparison, I used these two tools.

```
        this.subscribers = [];

        if (!this.silent) {
        }

        var onsubscribeType = "_YUICEOnSubscribe";
        if (type !== onsubscribeType) {
            this.subscribeEvent =
                    new YAHOO.util.CustomEvent(onsubscribeType, this, true);

        }
    };
```

The same function passed through JSMin has all unneeded whitespace removed:

```
YAHOO.util.CustomEvent=function(type,oScope,silent,signature){this.type=type;this.
scope=oScope||window;this.silent=silent;this.signature=signature||YAHOO.util.
CustomEvent.LIST;this.subscribers=[];if(!this.silent){}
var onsubscribeType="_YUICEOnSubscribe";if(type!==onsubscribeType){this.subscribeEv
ent=new YAHOO.util.CustomEvent(onsubscribeType,this,true);}};
```

Dojo Compressor removes most whitespace, but additionally shortens variable names. Notice how `_1` has replaced type as the first parameter to the `CustomEvent` function:

```
YAHOO.util.CustomEvent=function(_1,_2,_3,_4){
this.type=_1;
this.scope=_2||window;
this.silent=_3;
this.signature=_4||YAHOO.util.CustomEvent.LIST;
this.subscribers=[];
if(!this.silent){
}
var _5="_YUICEOnSubscribe";
if(_1!==_5){
this.subscribeEvent=new YAHOO.util.CustomEvent(_5,this,true);
}
};
```

Table 10-2 shows some potential savings for the six companies who didn't minify their JavaScript files. I downloaded the JavaScript files used on each site's home page. The table shows the original size of each site's JavaScript files, as well as the size reductions gained by running them through JSMin and Dojo Compressor. On average, JSMin reduced the size of JavaScript files by 21%, while Dojo Compressor achieved a 25% reduction.

Table 10-2. Size reductions from using JSMin and Dojo Compressor

Web site	Original size	JSMin savings	Dojo Compressor savings
http://www.amazon.com/	204K	31K (15%)	48K (24%)
http://www.aol.com/	44K	4K (10%)	4K (10%)
http://www.cnn.com/	98K	19K (20%)	24K (25%)
http://www.myspace.com/	88K	23K (27%)	24K (28%)
http://www.wikipedia.org/	42K	14K (34%)	16K (38%)
http://www.youtube.com/	34K	8K (22%)	10K (29%)
Average	85K	17K (21%)	21K (25%)

At what point do the additional savings from obfuscation justify the additional risks? Looking at these six examples, I would argue that all of them should simply minify their JavaScript code, thus avoiding the possible problems that obfuscation can cause. The one exception is Amazon, where an additional 17K (9%) would be saved by using obfuscation. A select few properties at Yahoo!, with large JavaScript payloads (>100K) obfuscate their JavaScript code. As we'll see below, the delta between minification and obfuscation decreases when combined with gzip compression.

Examples

To demonstrate the benefits of minification and obfuscation, I have generated two scripts of different sizes: a small script (50K) and a large script (377K). The small script drops to 13K after minification and 12K after obfuscation. The large script is reduced to 129K after minification and 123K after obfuscation. Testing both files under these three states results in the following six examples.

Small Script Normal
: *http://stevesouders.com/hpws/js-small-normal.php*

Small Script Minified
: *http://stevesouders.com/hpws/js-small-minify.php*

Small Script Obfuscated
: *http://stevesouders.com/hpws/js-small-obfuscate.php*

Large Script Normal
: *http://stevesouders.com/hpws/js-large-normal.php*

Large Script Minified
: *http://stevesouders.com/hpws/js-large-minify.php*

Large Script Obfuscated
: *http://stevesouders.com/hpws/js-large-obfuscate.php*

Script size	Normal	Minified	Obfuscated
Small (50K)	581 ms	481 ms	471 ms
Large (377K)	1092 ms	761 ms	751 ms

As mentioned in the previous section, the difference between minification and obfuscation decreases when combined with gzip compression; this is demonstrated by these examples. Minifying scripts reduces response times without carrying the risks that come with obfuscation.

Icing on the Cake

There are a couple other ways to squeeze waste out of your JavaScript.

Inline Scripts

The discussion thus far has focused on external JavaScript files. Inline JavaScript blocks should also be minified, though this practice is less evident on today's web sites. Table 10-4 shows that although 4 of the 10 top web sites minify their external scripts, only 3 minify their inline scripts.

Table 10-4. Inline minification practices across 10 top web sites

Web site	External scripts minified?	Inline scripts minified?
http://www.amazon.com	no	no
http://www.aol.com	no	no
http://www.cnn.com	no	no
http://www.ebay.com	yes	no
http://froogle.google.com	yes	yes
http://www.msn.com	yes	yes
http://www.myspace.com	no	no
http://www.wikipedia.org	no	no
http://www.yahoo.com	yes	yes
http://www.youtube.com	no	no

In practice, minifying inline scripts is easier than minifying external scripts. Whatever page generation platform you use (PHP, Python, Perl CGI, etc.), there is probably a version of JSMin that can be integrated with it. Once the functionality is available, all inlined JavaScript can be minified before being echoed to the HTML document.

Gzip and Minification

Rule 4 stresses the importance of compressing content and recommends using gzip to accomplish this, resulting in a typical size reduction of 70%. Gzip compression decreases file sizes more than minification—that's why it's in Rule 4 and this is Rule 10. I've heard people question whether minification is even worthwhile if gzip compression has already been enabled.

Table 10-5 is similar to Table 10-2, except the responses are gzipped. When gzipped, the average size of the JavaScript payload drops from 85K (see Table 10-2) to 23K (see Table 10-5), a reduction of 73%. It's reassuring to see that the guidelines of Rule 4 hold true for these six web sites. Table 10-5 shows that minifying the files in addition to gzipping them reduces the payload by an average of 4K (20%) over gzip alone. It's interesting that obfuscation and gzip perform about the same as minification and gzip, another reason to just stick with minification and avoid the additional risks of obfuscation.

Table 10-5. Size reductions with JSMin and Dojo Compressor after gzip compression

Web site	Original size after gzip	JSMin savings after gzip	Dojo Compressor savings after gzip
http://www.amazon.com	48K	7K (16%)	6K (13%)
http://www.aol.com	16K	1K (8%)	1K (8%)
http://www.cnn.com	29K	6K (19%)	6K (20%)
http://www.myspace.com	23K	4K (19%)	4K (19%)
http://www.wikipedia.org	13K	5K (37%)	5K (39%)
http://www.youtube.com	10K	2K (19%)	2K (20%)
Average	23K	4K (20%)	4K (20%)

In summary, the main numbers to compare are:

- 85K: JavaScript size without JSMin and gzip compression
- 68K: JavaScript size with only JSMin (21% savings)
- 23K: JavaScript size with only gzip compression (73% savings)
- 19K: JavaScript size with JSMin and gzip compression (78% savings)

CSS generally has fewer comments and less whitespace than JavaScript. The greatest potential for size savings comes from optimizing CSS—merging identical classes, removing unused classes, etc. This is a complex problem, given the order-dependent nature of CSS (the essence of why it's called *cascading*). This area warrants further research and tool development. The best solution might be one that removes comments and whitespace, and does straightforward optimizations such as using abbreviations (like "#606" instead of "#660066") and removing unnecessary strings ("0" instead of "0px").

Minify your JavaScript source code.

CHAPTER 11

Rule 11: Avoid Redirects

A *redirect* is used to reroute users from one URL to another. There are different kinds of redirects—301 and 302 are the most popular. Redirects are usually done for HTML documents, but they may also be used when requesting components in the page (images, scripts, etc.). There are different reasons for implementing redirects, including web site redesign, tracking traffic flow, counting ad impressions, and creating URLs that are easier for users to remember. We'll examine all of these aspects in this chapter, but the main thing to remember is that *redirects make your pages slower*.

Types of Redirects

When web servers return a redirect to the browser, the response has a status code in the 3xx range. This indicates that further action is required of the user agent in order to fulfill the request. There are several 3xx status codes:

- 300 Multiple Choices (based on Content-Type)
- 301 Moved Permanently
- 302 Moved Temporarily (a.k.a. Found)
- 303 See Other (clarification of 302)
- 304 Not Modified
- 305 Use Proxy
- 306 (no longer used)
- 307 Temporary Redirect (clarification of 302)

"304 Not Modified" is not really a redirect—it's used in response to conditional GET requests to avoid downloading data that is already cached by the browser, as explained in Chapter B. Status code 306 is deprecated.

The browser automatically takes the user to the URL specified in the Location field. All the information necessary for a redirect is in the headers. The body of the response is typically empty. Despite their names, neither a 301 nor a 302 response is cached in practice unless additional headers, such as Expires or Cache-Control, indicate that it should be.

There are other ways to automatically redirect users to a different URL. The meta refresh tag included in the head of an HTML document redirects the user after the number of seconds specified in the content attribute:

```
<meta http-equiv="refresh" content="0; url=http://stevesouders.com/newuri">
```

JavaScript is also used to perform redirects by setting the document.location to the desired URL. If you must do a redirect, the preferred technique is to use the standard 3xx HTTP status codes, primarily to ensure the Back button works correctly. For more information about this, see the W3C web article "Use standard redirects: don't break the back button!" at *http://www.w3.org/QA/Tips/reback*.

How Redirects Hurt Performance

Figure 11-1 shows how redirects slow down the user experience. The first HTTP request is the redirect. Nothing is displayed to the user until the redirect is completed and the HTML document is downloaded.

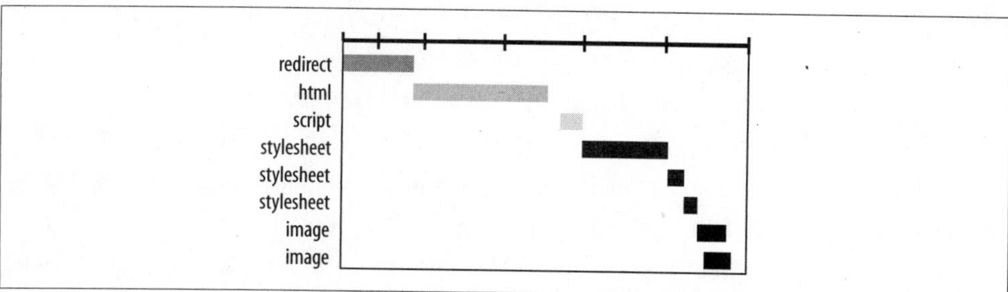

Figure 11-1. Redirects slow down web pages

In Chapter 5, I talk about the importance of downloading stylesheets quickly; otherwise, the page is blocked from rendering. Similarly, Chapter 6 explains how external scripts block the page from rendering and inhibit parallel downloads. The delays caused by redirects are even worse because they delay the delivery of the entire HTML document. Nothing in the page can be rendered and no components can be downloaded until the HTML document has arrived. Inserting a redirect between the user and the HTML document delays everything in the page.

Redirects are typically used with requests for the HTML document, but occasionally you'll see them used for components in the page. Figure 11-2 shows the HTTP requests for Google Toolbar. It contains four redirects.

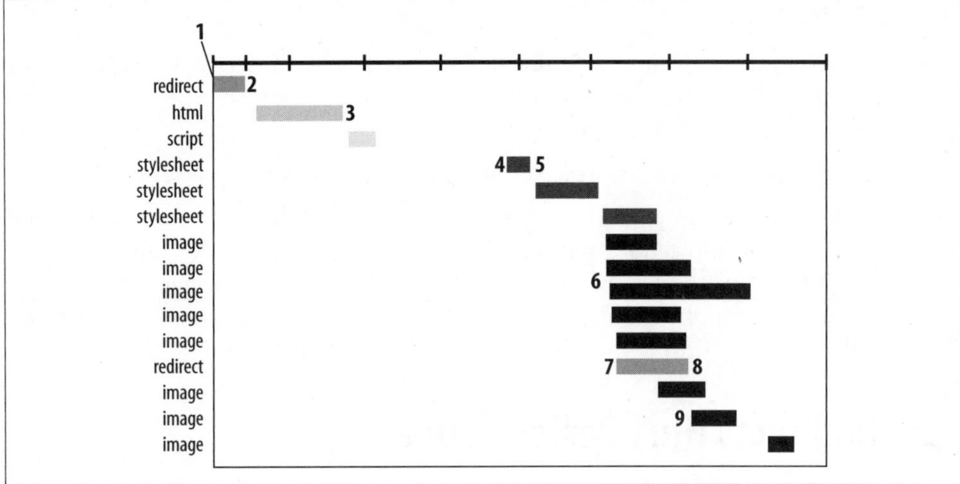

Figure 11-2. Multiple redirects including an image

The sequence of requests and redirects is complex, so I'll walk through them one at a time:

1. The initial URL *http://toolbar.google.com* is requested.
2. A 302 response is received with a `Location` of *http://toolbar.google.com/T4*.
3. *http://toolbar.google.com/T4/* is requested.
4. This HTML document redirects the user to *http://www.google.com/tools/firefox/toolbar/index.html* using JavaScript.
5. The JavaScript redirect results in a 302 response with the `Location` *http://www.google.com/tools/firefox/toolbar/FT3/intl/en/index.html*. At this point there have been a total of three redirects—one done with JavaScript and two using the 302 status code.
6. Six images are downloaded.
7. A seventh image is requested at *http://toolbar.google.com/T3/intl/search.gif*.

shows that 7 out of 10 top U.S. web sites use redirects—2 on the initial page and 5 when you navigate to secondary pages. Perhaps one or more of the redirects in the Google Toolbar page could have been avoided. Let's look at some typical uses of redirects and alternatives that don't have such a negative impact on end user response times.

Table 11-1. Redirects used across 10 top web sites

Web site	Uses redirects
http://www.amazon.com	No
http://www.aol.com	Yes—secondary page
http://www.cnn.com	Yes—initial page
http://www.ebay.com	Yes—secondary page
http://www.google.com	No
http://www.msn.com	Yes—initial page
http://www.myspace.com	Yes—secondary page
http://www.wikipedia.org	Yes—secondary page
http://www.yahoo.com	Yes—secondary page
http://www.youtube.com	No

Alternatives to Redirects

Redirects are an easy way to solve many problems, but it's better to use alternative solutions that don't slow down page loading. The following sections discuss some of the typical situations in which redirects are used, and alternatives that are better for your users.

Missing Trailing Slash

One of the most wasteful redirects happens frequently and web developers are generally not aware of it. It occurs when a trailing slash (/) is missing from a URL that should otherwise have one. For example, the redirect illustrated in Figure 11-1 was generated by going to *http://astrology.yahoo.com/astrology*. This request results in a 301 response containing a redirect to *http://astrology.yahoo.com/astrology/*. The only difference is the addition of a trailing slash.

There are good reasons for sending a redirect when the trailing slash is missing: it allows autoindexing (going to the index.html by default) and makes it possible to retrieve URLs in the page that are relative to the current directory (e.g., *logo.gif*). However, many popular web pages don't rely on autoindexing, instead relying on specific URLs and handlers. Additionally, URLs are often relative to the root and not to the current directory.

Note that a redirect does not happen if the trailing slash is missing after the hostname. For example, *http://www.yahoo.com* does not generate a redirect. However, the resultant URL seen in your browser does contain the trailing slash: *http://www.yahoo.com/*. The automatic appearance of the trailing slash is caused because the browser must specify some path when it makes the GET request. If there is no path, as in *http://www.yahoo.com*, then it uses simply the document root (/):

```
GET / HTTP/1.1
```

Sending a redirect when a trailing slash is missing is the default behavior for many web servers, including Apache. The `Alias` directive is an easy workaround. Another alternative is to use the `mod_rewrite` module, but `Alias` is simpler.* The problem with the Astrology site could be resolved by adding the following to the Apache configuration:

```
Alias /astrology /usr/local/apache/htdocs/astrology/index.html
```

If you're using handlers in Apache 2.0, a cleaner solution is available in the form of the `DirectorySlash` directive (for more information, visit *http://httpd.apache.org/docs/2.0/mod/mod_dir.html*). Assuming there is a handler named `astrologyhandler`, the use of `DirectorySlash` would look as follows:

```
<Location /astrology>
  DirectorySlash Off
  SetHandler astrologyhandler
</Location>
```

None of these alternatives solves the problem of finding URLs relative to the current directory, so the URLs of components in the page should be made relative to the root. Also, make sure you understand the order in which various modules are run (notably `mod_dir` and `mod_autoindex`) because using `DirectorySlash` this way could have security implications.

In summary, if your web site contains directories and uses autoindexing, it is likely that users are suffering a redirect to reach the intended page. You can check your web logs to see how many 301 status codes were issued, which can help you determine whether it is worthwhile to fix the missing trailing slash problem.

* For more information about the Apache `mod_rewrite` module, visit *http://httpd.apache.org/docs/1.3/mod/mod_rewrite.html*.

use for redirects. Others include connecting different parts of a web site and directing the user based on certain conditions (type of browser, type of user account, etc.). Using a redirect to connect two web sites is simple and requires little additional coding.

Several of the redirects in the Google Toolbar page load (shown in Figure 11-2) are used for just this purpose—to connect web sites. There are different parts of the backend web site (*T4*, *firefox*, and *FT3*). As new versions of the backend components are released (such as *T5* and *FT4*), they can be linked to the main web site by simply updating the redirects.

Although redirects reduce the complexity for developers, it degrades the user experience, as described in the earlier section "How Redirects Hurt Performance." There are alternatives for integrating two backends that, while creating more work for developers than a simple redirect, are not daunting and improve the user experience:

- `Alias`, `mod_rewrite`, and `DirectorySlash` (described previously in the "Missing Trailing Slash" section) require committing to an interface (handlers or filenames) in addition to URLs, but are simple to implement.
- If the two backends reside on the same server, it's likely that the code itself could be linked. For example, the older handler code could call the new handler code programmatically.
- If the domain name changes, a CNAME (a DNS record that creates an alias pointing from one domain name to another) can be used to make both hostnames point to the same server(s). If this is possible, the techniques mentioned here (`Alias`, `mod_rewrite`, `DirectorySlash`, and directly linking code) are viable.

Tracking Internal Traffic

Redirects are often used to track the flow of user traffic. This is seen on the Yahoo! home page (*http://www.yahoo.com*) where many of the navigation links are wrapped by a redirect. For example, the URL for the Sports link is *http://www.yahoo.com/r/26*. Clicking on this link results in a 301 response with the `Location` set to *http://sports.yahoo.com/*. The traffic patterns of people leaving Yahoo!'s home page can be discerned by analyzing the web server logs from *www.yahoo.com*. In this case, the number of people leaving to go to Yahoo! Sports is equal to the number of `/r/26` entries in the logs.

An alternative is to use *Referer*[*] logging to track traffic patterns. Every HTTP request contains the URL of the page from which it was generated, i.e., the referer (in some cases there is no referring page, such as when the user types the URL or uses bookmarks). In this example, when the user navigates to the Sports page from the Yahoo! home page, the access logs from *sports.yahoo.com* contain a Referer value of *http://www.yahoo.com/*. Using Referer logging avoids sending the user through a redirect, thus improving response times. The difficulty with this approach, however, is that for Yahoo! home page to gather statistics on everyone leaving its site, Yahoo! has to analyze the logs of all the destination web sites (Sports, Mail, Calendar, Movies, etc.).

For internal traffic—i.e., traffic from web sites within the same company—it's worthwhile to avoid redirects by setting up Referer logging to improve end user response times. If the destination web site belongs to a different company, it might not be possible to analyze the logs for Referers. This situation is discussed in the next section.

Tracking Outbound Traffic

When you're trying to track user traffic, you might find that links are taking users away from your web site. In this situation, the use of Referer is not practical.

This is the situation faced by Yahoo! Search. Yahoo! solves the tracking problem by wrapping each search result link in a redirect. The URL of the search result goes to *rds.yahoo.com* and contains the ultimate destination as a parameter in the URL. For example, here's a search result link going to the entry for "Performance" at Wikipedia:

```
http://rds.yahoo.com/[...]5742/**http%3a//en.wikipedia.org/wiki/Performance
```

Clicking on this search result accesses *rds.yahoo.com*, which returns a 302 response with the `Location` set to *http://en.wikipedia.org/wiki/Performance*. Administrators can then track where users are going by analyzing the ** parameters from web server logs on *rds.yahoo.com*. The redirect slows retrieval of the destination page, which has a negative impact on the user's experience.

An alternative to redirects for outbound traffic is to use a *beacon*—an HTTP request that contains tracking information in the URL. The tracking information is extracted from the access logs on the beacon web server(s). The beacon response is typically a one-pixel by one-pixel transparent image, although a 204 response is a more elegant solution because it's smaller, never cached, and by definition does not alter the state of the browser.

In the case of Yahoo! Search, the goal would be to send a beacon whenever the user clicks on a search result link. This is done using the `onclick` handler for each link (when JavaScript is enabled). The `onclick` handler calls a JavaScript function that

[*] This misspelling of "referrer" is so prevalent that it became part of the HTTP specification.

```
    beacon.src = "http://rds.yahoo.com/?url=" + escape(anchor.href);
}
</script>
```

Be warned: beacons have a number of nuances that make reliable implementation challenging. The challenge in this situation is the race condition between sending the beacon while the page itself is being unloaded. The image beacon's `onload` handler can be used to ensure the beacon has been delivered before unloading the document:

```
<a href="http://en.wikipedia.org/wiki/Performance"
   onclick="resultBeacon(this); return false;">Performance - Wikipedia</a>

<script type="text/javascript">
var beacon;
function resultBeacon(anchor) {
    beacon = new Image( );
    beacon.onload = gotoUrl;
    beacon.onerror = gotoUrl;
    beacon.anchor = anchor;
    beacon.src = "http://rds.yahoo.com/?url=" + escape(anchor.href);
}

function gotoUrl( ) {
    document.location = beacon.anchor.href;
}
</script>
```

This approach is likely to be as slow as using a redirect because both techniques require an additional HTTP request. Another approach is to use `XMLHttpRequest` to send the beacon, but to only wait until the request reaches `readyState 2` (sent) before unloading the page. This is faster than waiting for the entire HTTP response of a redirect, but you'll have to decide whether the complexity is justified. For more information about using XMLHttpRequest, visit *http://www.w3.org/TR/XMLHttpRequest*. A code sample is too complex to show here, but you can see one in the "XMLHttp-Request Beacon" example. There is also an example of the more typical image beacon.

XMLHttpRequest Beacon
: *http://stevesouders.com/hpws/xhr-beacon.php*

Image Beacon
: *http://stevesouders.com/hpws/redir-beacon.php*

Even if these approaches are too complex for most links, they work well for links that use the `target` attribute:

```
<a href="http://en.wikipedia.org/wiki/Performance"
   onclick="resultBeacon(this)"
   target="_blank">Performance - Wikipedia</a>
```

In this case, there is no race condition and a simple image beacon works fine. This approach works well, for example, when tracking impressions (clicks) for pop-up ads. Clicking on a pop-up ad does not unload the current document, allowing the image beacon request to be completed without interruption.

Prettier URLs

Another motivation for redirects is to make URLs prettier and easier to remember. In the earlier "Missing Trailing Slash" section, I explained how *http://astrology.yahoo.com/astrology* redirects the user to *http://astrology.yahoo.com/astrology/* (the same URL with a "/" appended). A redirect that affects far more users is from *http://astrology.yahoo.com* to *http://astrology.yahoo.com/astrology/*. Clearly, *http://astrology.yahoo.com* is prettier and easier to remember, so it's good for users that this simple URL works.

The Google Toolbar redirects described in the "How Redirects Hurt Performance" section are another example of using redirects to support a prettier and easier-to-remember URL. Imagine how difficult it would be to type or remember *http://www.google.com/tools/firefox/toolbar/FT3/intl/en/index.html*. It's much easier to remember *http://toolbar.google.com*.

The key is to find a way to have these simpler URLs without the redirects. Rather than forcing users to undergo an additional HTTP request, it would be better to avoid the redirect using `Alias`, `mod_rewrite`, `DirectorySlash`, and directly linking code, as described in the earlier section "Connecting Web Sites."

> **Find ways to avoid redirects.**

It hurts performance to include the same JavaScript file twice in one page. This mistake isn't as unusual as you might think. A review of the 10 top U.S. web sites shows that two of them (CNN and YouTube) contain a duplicated script.

How does this happen? How does it affect performance? How can it be avoided? Let's take a look.

Duplicate Scripts—They Happen

Two main factors increase the odds of a script being duplicated in a single web page: team size and number of scripts.

It takes a significant amount of resources to develop a web site, especially if it's a top destination. In addition to the core team building the site, other teams contribute to the HTML in the page for things such as advertising, branding (logos, headers, footers, etc.), and data feeds (news stories, sports scores, TV listings, etc.). With so many people from different teams adding HTML to the page, it's easy to imagine how the same script could be added twice. For example, two developers might be contributing JavaScript code that requires manipulating cookies, so each of them includes the company's *cookies.js* script. Both developers are unaware that the other has already added the script to the page.

As shown in Table 12-1, the average number of scripts in the 10 top U.S. sites is greater than six (this information is also given in Table 1-1 from Chapter 1). The two sites that have duplicate scripts also happen to have an above-average number of scripts (CNN has 11; YouTube has 7). The more scripts in the page, the more likely it is that one of the scripts will be included twice.

Table 12-1. Number of scripts and stylesheets for 10 top sites

Web site	Scripts	Stylesheets
http://www.amazon.com	3	1
http://www.aol.com	18	1
http://www.cnn.com	11	2
http://www.bay.com	7	2
http://froogle.google.com	1	1
http://www.msn.com	9	1
http://www.myspace.com	2	2
http://www.wikipedia.org	3	1
http://www.yahoo.com	4	1
http://www.youtube.com	7	3

Duplicate Scripts Hurt Performance

There are two ways that duplicate scripts hurt performance: unnecessary HTTP requests and wasted JavaScript execution.

Unnecessary HTTP requests happen in Internet Explorer, but not in Firefox. In Internet Explorer, if an external script is included twice and is not cacheable, the browser generates two HTTP requests during page loading. This is demonstrated in the "Duplicate Scripts—Not Cached" example.

Duplicate Scripts—Not Cached
http://stevesouders.com/hpws/dupe-scripts.php

This won't be an issue for people who follow the advice in Chapter 3 and add a far future `Expires` header to their scripts, but if they don't, and they make the mistake of including the script twice, the user has to endure an extra HTTP request. Chapter 6 explains how downloading scripts has an especially negative impact on response times. Subjecting the user to an extra HTTP request for a script doubles that negative impact.

Even if the script is cacheable, extra HTTP requests occur when the user reloads the page. The following example includes scripts that are cacheable.

Duplicate Scripts—Cached
http://stevesouders.com/hpws/dupe-scripts-cached.php

Load this page once to fill the cache, and then click the "Example 2 – Duplicate Scripts – Cached" link to load it again. Since the script is cached, no HTTP requests are made for the script, but if you click the browser's Refresh button, two HTTP requests are made. Specifically, two conditional GET requests are made. For more information, see the section "Conditional GET Requests" in Chapter B.

instance of a script in the page. In the following example, the same script is included 10 times, which results in 10 evaluations. When you reload the page, 10 HTTP requests are made (only in Internet Explorer).

Duplicate Scripts—10 Cached

http://stevesouders.com/hpws/dupe-scripts-cached10.php

To summarize:

- Including the same script multiple times in a page makes it slower.
- In Internet Explorer, extra HTTP requests are made if the script is not cacheable or when the page is reloaded.
- In both Firefox and Internet Explorer, the script is evaluated multiple times.

Avoiding Duplicate Scripts

One way to avoid accidentally including the same script twice is to implement a script management module in your templating system. The typical way to include a script is to use the `SCRIPT` tag in your HTML page:

```
<script type="text/javascript" src="menu_1.0.17.js"></script>
```

An alternative in PHP would be to create a function called `insertScript`:

```
<?php insertScript("menu.js") ?>
```

While we're tackling the duplicate script issue, we'll add functionality to handle dependencies and versioning of scripts. A simple implementation of `insertScript` follows:

```
<?php
function insertScript($jsfile) {
    if ( alreadyInserted($jsfile) ) {
        return;
    }
    pushInserted($jsfile);

    if ( hasDependencies($jsfile) ) {
        $dependencies = getDependencies($jsfile);
        Foreach ($dependencies as $script) {
            insertScript($script);
        }
    }
```

```
        echo '<script type="text/javascript" src="' . getVersion($jsfile) . '"></script>
";
    }
    ?>
```

The first time a script is inserted, we'll reach pushInserted. This adds the script to the alreadyInserted list for the page. If that script is accidentally inserted again, the test for alreadyInserted will not add the script again, thus solving the duplicate script issue.

If this script has dependencies, those prerequisite scripts are inserted. In this example, *menu.js* might depend on *events.js* and *utils.js*. You can capture these dependency relationships using a hash or database. For simpler sites, dependencies can be maintained manually. For more complex sites, you may choose to automate the generation of dependencies by scanning the scripts to find symbol definitions.

Finally, the script is echoed to the page. A key function here is getVersion. This function looks up the script (in this case *menu.js*) and returns the filename with the appropriate version appended (e.g., *menu_1.0.17.js*). In Chapter 3, I mention the advantage of adding a version number to a component's filename; when using a far future Expires header the filename has to be changed whenever the file contents are changed (see the section "Revving Filenames" in Chapter 3). Centralizing this functionality inside insertScript is another benefit of this script management module. Whenever a script is modified, all the pages start using the new filename after a simple update to the getVersion code. Pages start using the new version immediately without having to modify any of the PHP templates.

Make sure scripts are included only once.

Reducing the number of HTTP requests necessary to render your page is the best way to accelerate the user experience. You can achieve this by maximizing the browser's ability to cache your components, but the `ETag` header thwarts caching when a web site is hosted on more than one server. In this chapter, I explain what ETags are and how their default implementation slows down web pages.

What's an ETag?

Entity tags (ETags) are a mechanism that web servers and browsers use to validate cached components. Before jumping into the details of ETags, let's review how components are cached and validated.

Expires Header

As the browser downloads components, it stores them in its cache. On subsequent page views, if the cached component is "fresh," the browser reads it from disk and avoids making an HTTP request. A component is fresh if it hasn't expired, based on the value in the `Expires` header. Let's look at an example.

When a component is requested, the server of origin has the option to send an `Expires` header back in the response:

```
Expires: Thu, 15 Apr 2010 20:00:00 GMT
```

Chapter 3 recommends setting an expiration date in the far future. How far is "far" depends on the component in question. An ad image might have to expire daily, whereas a company logo could expire in 10 years. The HTTP specification (*http://www.w3.org/Protocols/rfc2616/rfc2616-sec14.html#sec14.21*) suggests servers should not set an `Expires` date more than one year in the future, but this is a guideline; browsers support `Expires` dates further in the future than one year. It's most efficient to avoid HTTP requests by setting the expiration date so far in the future that the components are unlikely to expire.

Conditional GET Requests

In the event a cached component does expire (or the user explicitly reloads the page), the browser can't reuse it without first checking that it is still valid. This is called a *conditional GET request* (see the section "Conditional GET Requests" in Chapter B). It's unfortunate that the browser has to make this HTTP request to perform a validity check, but it's more efficient than simply downloading every component that has expired. If the component in the browser's cache is valid (i.e., it matches what's on the origin server), instead of returning the entire component, the origin server returns a "304 Not Modified" status code.

There are two ways in which the server determines whether the cached component matches the one on the origin server:

- By comparing the last-modified date
- By comparing the entity tag

Last-Modified Date

The component's last-modified date is returned by the origin server via the `Last-Modified` response header.

```
GET /i/yahoo.gif HTTP/1.1
Host: us.yimg.com
```

```
HTTP/1.1 200 OK
Last-Modified: Tue, 12 Dec 2006 03:03:59 GMT
Content-Length: 1195
```

In this example, the browser caches the component (in this case, the Yahoo! logo) along with its last-modified date. The next time *http://us.yimg.com/i/yahoo.gif* is requested, the browser uses the `If-Modified-Since` header to pass the last-modified date back to the origin server for comparison. If the last-modified date on the origin server matches that sent by the browser, a 304 response is returned and the 1195 bytes of data don't have to be sent.

```
GET /i/yahoo.gif HTTP/1.1
Host: us.yimg.com
If-Modified-Since: Tue, 12 Dec 2006 03:03:59 GMT
```

```
HTTP/1.1 304 Not Modified
```

```
GET /i/yahoo.gif HTTP/1.1
Host: us.yimg.com
```

```
HTTP/1.1 200 OK
Last-Modified: Tue, 12 Dec 2006 03:03:59 GMT
ETag: "10c24bc-4ab-457e1c1f"
Content-Length: 1195
```

ETags were added to provide a more flexible mechanism for validating entities than the last-modified date. If, for example, an entity changes based on the `User-Agent` or `Accept-Language` headers, the state of the entity can be reflected in the ETag.

Later, if the browser has to validate a component, it uses the `If-None-Match` header to pass the ETag back to the origin server. If the ETags match, a 304 status code is returned, reducing the response by 1195 bytes.

```
GET /i/yahoo.gif HTTP/1.1
Host: us.yimg.com
If-Modified-Since: Tue, 12 Dec 2006 03:03:59 GMT
If-None-Match: "10c24bc-4ab-457e1c1f"
```

```
HTTP/1.1 304 Not Modified
```

The Problem with ETags

The problem with ETags is that they are typically constructed using attributes that make them unique to a specific server hosting a site. ETags won't match when a browser gets the original component from one server and later makes a conditional GET request that goes to a different server—a situation that is all too common on web sites that use a cluster of servers to handle requests. By default, both Apache and IIS embed data in the ETag that dramatically reduces the odds of the validity test succeeding on web sites with multiple servers.

The ETag format for Apache 1.3 and 2.x is `inode-size-timestamp`. Inodes are used by filesystems to store information such as file type, owner, group, and access mode. Although a given file may reside in the same directory across multiple servers and have the same file size, permissions, timestamp, etc., its inode is different from one server to the next.

IIS 5.0 and 6.0 have a similar issue with ETags. The format for ETags on IIS is `Filetimestamp:ChangeNumber`. `ChangeNumber` is a counter used to track configuration changes to IIS. It's unlikely that the `ChangeNumber` is the same across all IIS servers behind a web site.

The end result is that ETags generated by Apache and IIS for the exact same component won't match from one server to another. If the ETags don't match, the user doesn't receive the small, fast 304 response that ETags were designed for; instead, they'll get a normal 200 response along with all the data for the component. If you host your web site on just one server, this isn't a problem, but if you use a cluster of servers, components have to be downloaded much more often than is required, which degrades performance.

The unnecessary reloading of components also has a performance impact on your servers and increases your bandwidth costs. If you have *n* servers in your cluster in round-robin rotation, the probability that the ETag in the user's cache will match the server they land on next is *1/n*. If you have 10 servers, the user has a 10% chance of getting the correct 304 response, leaving a 90% chance of getting a wasteful 200 response and full data download.

This ETag issue also degrades the effectiveness of proxy caches. The ETag cached by users behind the proxy frequently won't match the ETag cached by the proxy, resulting in unnecessary requests back to the origin server. Instead of one 304 response between the user and the proxy, there are two (slower, bigger) 200 responses: one from the origin server to the proxy, and another from the proxy to the user. The default format of ETags has also been cited as a possible security vulnerability.*

It gets worse.

The `If-None-Match` header takes precedence over `If-Modified-Since`. You might hope that if the ETags didn't match but the last-modified date was the same, a "304 Not Modified" response would be sent, but that's not the case. According to the HTTP/1.1 specification (*http://www.w3.org/Protocols/rfc2616/rfc2616-sec13.html#sec13.3.4*), if both of these headers are in the request, the origin server "MUST NOT return a response status of 304 (Not Modified) unless doing so is consistent with all of the conditional header fields in the request." It would actually be better if the `If-None-Match` header wasn't even there. That's the solution discussed in the next section.

* See the "Apache http daemon file inode disclosure vulnerability" web article at *http://www3.ca.com/securityadvisor/vulninfo/vuln.aspx?ID=7196* for more information.

Even if your components have a far future `Expires` header, a conditional GET request is still made whenever the user clicks Reload or Refresh. There's no way around it—the problem with ETags has to be addressed.

One option is to configure your ETags to take advantage of their flexible validation capabilities. One example might be a script that varies depending on whether the browser is Internet Explorer. Using PHP to generate the script, you could set the `ETag` header to reflect the browser state:

```
<?php
if ( strpos($_SERVER["HTTP_USER_AGENT"], "MSIE") ) {
    header("ETag: MSIE");
}
else {
    header("ETag: notMSIE");
}
?>
```

If you have components that have to be validated based on something other than the last-modified date, ETags are a powerful way of doing that.

If you don't have the need to customize ETags, it is best to simply remove them. Both Apache and IIS have identified ETags as a performance issue, and suggest changing the contents of the Etag (see *http://www.apacheweek.com/issues/02-01-18*, *http://support.microsoft.com/?id=922733*, and *http://support.microsoft.com/kb/922703* for more details).

Apache versions 1.3.23 and later support the `FileETag` directive. With this directive, the `inode` value can be removed from the ETag, leaving size and timestamp as the remaining components of the ETag. Similarly, in IIS you can set the `ChangeNumber` to be identical across all servers, leaving the file timestamp as the only other piece of information in the ETag.

Following these suggestions leaves an ETag that contains just the size and timestamp (Apache) or just the timestamp (IIS). However, because this is basically duplicate information, it's better to just remove the ETag altogether—the `Last-Modified` header provides sufficiently equivalent information, and removing the ETag reduces the size of the HTTP headers in both the response and subsequent requests. The Microsoft Support articles referenced in this section describe how to remove ETags.

In Apache, you can remove Etags by simply adding the following line to your Apache configuration file:

```
FileETag none
```

ETags in the Real World

Table 13-1 shows that 6 out of 10 top U.S. web sites use ETags on a majority of their components. To be fair, three of them have modified the ETag format to remove `inode` (Apache) or `ChangeNumber` (IIS). Four or more contain ETags that haven't been modified and therefore cause the performance problems discussed previously.

Table 13-1. ETags observed across 10 top web sites

Web Site	Components with ETags	Fixed
http://www.amazon.com	0% (0/24)	n/a
http://www.aol.com	5% (3/63)	yes
http://www.cnn.com	83% (157/190)	no
http://www.ebay.com	86% (57/66)	no
http://www.google.com	0% (0/5)	n/a
http://www.msn.com	72% (42/58)	no
http://www.myspace.com	84% (32/38)	yes and no
http://www.wikipedia.org	94% (16/17)	unknown
http://www.yahoo.com	0% (0/34)	n/a
http://www.youtube.com	70% (43/61)	yes

An example of a component with different ETags across the cluster of servers is *http://stc.msn.com/br/hp/en-us/css/15/blu.css* from *http://msn.com*. The HTTP headers from the first request in the example contains an ETag value of `80b31d5a4776c71:6e0`.

```
GET /br/hp/en-us/css/15/blu.css HTTP/1.1
Host: stc.msn.com
```

```
HTTP/1.1 200 OK
Last-Modified: Tue, 03 Apr 2007 23:25:23 GMT
ETag: "80b31d5a4776c71:6e0"
Content-Length: 647
Server: Microsoft-IIS/6.0
```

On the first reload, the ETag matches and a 304 response is sent. The `Content-Length` header is missing from the response because the 304 status code tells the browser to use the content from its cache.

```
GET /br/hp/en-us/css/15/blu.css HTTP/1.1
Host: stc.msn.com
If-Modified-Since: Tue, 03 Apr 2007 23:25:23 GMT
If-None-Match: "80b31d5a4776c71:6e0"
```

```
If-Modified-Since: Tue, 03 Apr 2007 23:25:23 GMT
If-None-Match: "80b31d5a4776c71:6e0"
```

```
HTTP/1.1 200 OK
Last-Modified: Tue, 03 Apr 2007 23:25:23 GMT
ETag: "80b31d5a4776c71:47b"
Content-Length: 647
Server: Microsoft-IIS/6.0
```

Even though the ETag changed, we know this is the same component. The size (647 bytes) is the same. The last-modified date (03 April 2007 23:25:23) is the same. The ETags are almost the same. Let's look at the ETag headers more closely:

```
ETag: "80b31d5a4776c71:6e0"
ETag: "80b31d5a4776c71:47b"
```

The `Server` header in the response confirms that this is from IIS. As described earlier, the default ETag format for IIS is `Filetimestamp:ChangeNumber`. Both ETags have the same value for `Filetimestamp` (`80b31d5a4776c71`). This isn't a surprise because the `Last-Modified` header shows that both components have the same modification date. The `ChangeNumber` is the part of the ETag that differs. Although disappointing, this also isn't a surprise because, as stated in the Microsoft Support articles referenced earlier, this is precisely what causes the performance issues. Removing `ChangeNumber` from the ETag or removing the ETag altogether would avoid these unnecessary and inefficient downloads of data that's already in the browser's cache.

Reconfigure or remove ETags.

CHAPTER 14

Rule 14: Make Ajax Cacheable

People frequently ask whether the performance rules in this book apply to Web 2.0 applications. They definitely do! The rule discussed in this chapter is, however, the first rule that resulted from working with Web 2.0 applications at Yahoo!. In this chapter, I describe what Web 2.0 means, how Ajax fits into Web 2.0, and an important performance improvement you can make to Ajax.

Web 2.0, DHTML, and Ajax

The relationship between Web 2.0, DHTML, and Ajax is illustrated in Figure 14-1. This figure doesn't show that Ajax is used only in DHTML or that DHTML is used only by Web 2.0 applications, but rather it is meant to show that Web 2.0 includes many concepts, one of which is DHTML, and that Ajax is one of the key technologies in DHTML. A discussion of Web 2.0 and what it includes is a book (or more) by itself, but we do want to have a common understanding of these terms. Below, I give brief definitions with references for more information.

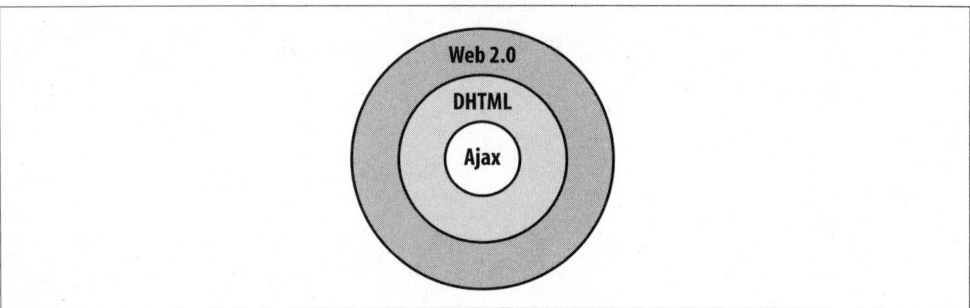

Figure 14-1. Relationship between Web 2.0, DHTML, and Ajax

more like an application with well-defined inputs and outputs. DHTML and Ajax are technologies for implementing these concepts. In his web article "Web 2.0 Compact Definition: Trying Again" (*http://radar.oreilly.com/archives/2006/12/web_20_compact.html*), Tim O'Reilly provides one of the most referenced definitions of Web 2.0.

DHTML

Dynamic HTML allows the presentation of an HTML page to change after the page has loaded. This is accomplished using JavaScript and CSS interacting with the Document Object Model (DOM) in the browser. Examples include links that change when the user hovers the mouse over them, tree controls that expand and collapse, and cascading menus within the page. More complex DHTML pages may redraw the entire page based on the user's intention; for example, changing from viewing an email inbox to a form for composing an email message. Ajax is a technology used in DHTML so that the client can retrieve and display new information requested by the user without reloading the page.

Ajax

The term "Ajax" was coined in 2005 by Jesse James Garrett.* Ajax stands for "Asynchronous JavaScript and XML" (although today there are alternatives to XML, most notably JSON). Ajax is not a single, licensable technology, but is instead a collection of technologies, primarily JavaScript, CSS, DOM, and asynchronous data retrieval. The goal of Ajax is to break out of the start-and-stop nature of interaction on the Web. Displaying a blank white screen to the user followed by repainting the entire window is not a good user experience. Instead, Ajax inserts a layer between the UI and web server. This Ajax layer resides on the client, interacting with the web server to get requested information, and interfacing with the presentation layer to update only the components necessary. It transforms the Web experience from "viewing pages" to "interacting with an application."

* Jesse James Garrett, "Ajax: A New Approach to Web Applications," *http://www.adaptivepath.com/publications/essays/archives/000385.php*.

The technologies behind Ajax have been around much longer than the phrase itself. IFrames, first found in Internet Explorer 3 in 1996, allow asynchronous loading of content within a page, and are still used today in some Ajax applications. `XMLHttpRequest`, what I consider the heart of Ajax, was available in Internet Explorer 5 in 1999 (under the name `XMLHTTP`), and in Mozilla in 2002. The proposed W3C XMLHttpRequest specification for Ajax was first released in April 2006.

I highly recommend using the Yahoo! UI (YUI) Connection Manager for Ajax development (*http://developer.yahoo.com/yui/connection*). It handles browser compatibility issues with `XMLHttpRequest` and has excellent documentation and code samples.

Asynchronous = Instantaneous?

One of the cited benefits of Ajax is that it provides instantaneous feedback to the user because it requests information asynchronously from the backend web server. In the article referenced earlier, Jesse James Garrett uses Google Suggest and Google Maps as examples of web interfaces where "everything happens almost instantly."

Be careful! Using Ajax is no guarantee that the user won't be twiddling his thumbs waiting for those "asynchronous JavaScript and XML" responses to return. I'd hate to use Google Maps and Yahoo! Maps on a dial-up connection. In many applications, whether or not the user is kept waiting depends on how Ajax is used. Frontend engineers once again shoulder the responsibility of identifying and following the best practices required to ensure a fast user experience.

A key factor to whether the user might be kept waiting is whether the Ajax requests are passive or active. *Passive requests* are made in anticipation of a future need. For example, in a web-based email client, a passive request might be used to download the user's address book before it's actually needed. By loading it passively, the client makes sure the address book is already in its cache when the user needs to address an email message. *Active requests* are made based on the user's current actions. An example is finding all the email messages that match the user's search criteria.

The latter example illustrates that even though active Ajax requests are asynchronous, the user may still be kept waiting for the response. It is true that, thanks to Ajax, the user won't have to endure a complete page reload, and the UI is still responsive while the user waits. Nevertheless, the user is most likely sitting, waiting for the search results to be displayed before taking any further action. It's important to remember that "asynchronous" does not imply "instantaneous." I definitely agree with Jesse James Garrett's final FAQ.

> Q. Do Ajax applications always deliver a better experience than traditional web applications?
>
> A. Not necessarily. Ajax gives interaction designers more flexibility. However, the more power we have, the more caution we must use in exercising it. We must be careful to use Ajax to enhance the user experience of our applications, not degrade it.

The previous section makes it clear that it's possible that the user will be kept waiting when making active Ajax requests. To improve performance, it's important to optimize these requests. The techniques for optimizing active Ajax requests are equally applicable to passive Ajax requests, but since active requests have a greater impact on the user experience, you should start with them.

To find all the active Ajax requests in your web application, start your favorite packet sniffer. (The section "How the Tests Were Done" in Chapter 15 mentions my favorite packet sniffer: IBM Page Detailer.) After your web application has loaded, start using it while watching for Ajax requests that show up in the packet sniffer. These are the active Ajax requests that have to be optimized for better performance.

The most important way to improve these active Ajax requests is to make the responses cacheable, as discussed in Chapter 3. Some of the other 13 rules we've already covered are also applicable to Ajax requests:

- Rule 4: Gzip Components
- Rule 9: Reduce DNS Lookups
- Rule 10: Minify JavaScript
- Rule 11: Avoid Redirects
- Rule 13: Configure ETags

However, Rule 3 is the most important. It might not be fair for me to create a new rule that simply reapplies previous rules in a new context, but I've found that, because Ajax is so new and different, these performance improvements have to be called out explicitly.

Caching Ajax in the Real World

Let's take a look at some examples to see how Ajax adheres to these performance guidelines in the real world.

Yahoo! Mail

In our first example, we'll look at the Ajax version of Yahoo! Mail (*http://mail.yahoo.com*), which is in beta at the time of this writing.

When the user starts the Ajax version of Yahoo! Mail, it downloads the body of the user's first three email messages. This is a smart passive Ajax request. There's a good chance the user will click on one or more of these email messages, so having them already downloaded in the client means that the user sees her email messages without having to wait for any Ajax responses.

If the user wants to view an email message that's not in the first three, an active Ajax request is made. The user is waiting for this response so she can read the email message. Let's look at the HTTP headers.

```
GET /ws/mail/v1/formrpc?m=GetMessage[snip...] HTTP/1.1
Host: us.mg0.mail.yahoo.com
Accept-Encoding: gzip,deflate
```

```
HTTP/1.1 200 OK
Date: Mon, 23 Apr 2007 23:22:57 GMT
Cache-Control: no-store, private
Expires: Thu, 01 Jan 1970 00:00:00 GMT
Content-Type: text/xml; charset=UTF-8
Content-Encoding: gzip
Connection: keep-alive
```

Now imagine that the user leaves Yahoo! Mail to visit another web site. Later, she returns to Yahoo! Mail and again clicks on the fourth email message. Not surprisingly, the exact same request is sent again because the previous Ajax response was not saved in the browser's cache. It wasn't cached because the response contains a `Cache-Control` header with the value `no-store`, and an `Expires` header with a date in the past. Both of these tell the browser not to cache the response. And yet, if her inbox hasn't changed, the content is identical in both responses.

If these headers were replaced with a far future `Expires` header (see Chapter 3) the response would be cached and read off disk, resulting in a faster user experience. This might seem counterintuitive to some developers—after all, this is a dynamically generated response that contains information relevant to only one user in the world. It doesn't seem to make sense to cache this data. The critical thing to remember is that this one user might make that request multiple times in a day or week. If you can make the response cacheable for her, it may make the difference between a slow user experience and a fast one.

Making this Ajax response cacheable requires more work than simply changing the HTTP headers. The personalized and dynamic nature of the response has to be reflected in what's cached. The best way to do this is with query string parameters. For example, this response is valid only for the current user. This can be addressed by putting the username in the query string:

```
/ws/mail/v1/formrpc?m=GetMessage&yid=steve_souders
```

It's also important that the exact message is reflected. We wouldn't want to say `&msg=4`, because what's "fourth" in the inbox is constantly changing. Instead, a message ID that is unique across all messages for this user would solve the problem:

A better alternative for handling data privacy is using a secure communications protocol such as Secure Sockets Layer (SSL). SSL responses are cacheable (only for the current browser session in Firefox), so it provides a compromise: data privacy is ensured while cached responses improve performance during the current session.

Walking through the other relevant performance rules, we can find several positive performance traits in this implementation. The response is gzipped (Rule 4). The domain is used in many other requests in the page, which helps to avoid additional DNS lookups (Rule 9). The XML response is minified as much as possible (Rule 10). It doesn't use redirects (Rule 11). And the ETags are removed (Rule 13).

Google Spreadsheets

Google Docs & Spreadsheets (*http://docs.google.com*) offers an Ajax spreadsheet application, which is in beta at the time of this writing.

In a typical workflow, the user creates a spreadsheet and saves it in his list of documents. Let's examine what happens when the user returns and opens the spreadsheet. Figure 14-2 shows the HTTP traffic when the spreadsheet is opened—10 active Ajax requests are made. On a side note, this illustrates that Ajax requests are not exclusively XML-fetched using `XMLHttpRequest`. In Google Spreadsheets, the Ajax requests are HTML and JavaScript. Some of these are requested using `XMLHttpRequest`, but IFrames are also used.

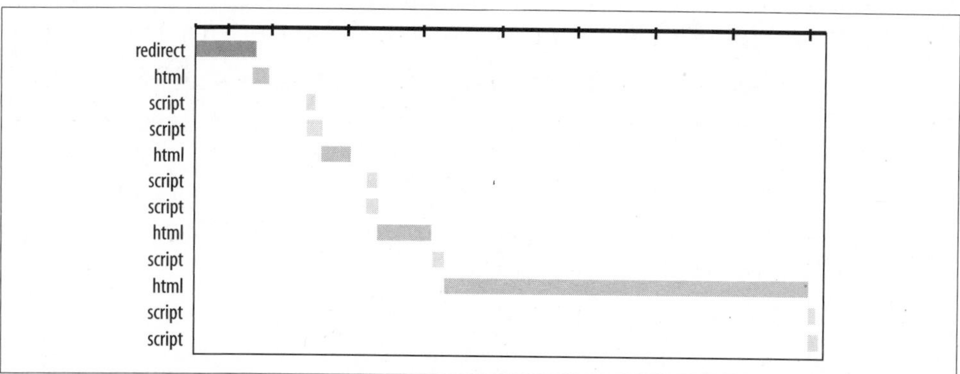

Figure 14-2. Active Ajax requests in Google Spreadsheets

If the user closes the spreadsheet and reopens it, 10 requests are made again. That's because none of the requests is cacheable. Most of the requests are fairly small, but one of the HTML requests is 47K (before compression). Let's look at the HTTP headers for that request.

```
GET /ar?id=[snip...]&srow=0&erow=100 HTTP/1.1
Host: spreadsheets.google.com
Accept-Encoding: gzip,deflate
```

```
HTTP/1.1 200 OK
Content-Type: text/html; charset=UTF-8
Cache-Control: private
Content-Encoding: gzip
Date: Tue, 24 Apr 2007 23:37:13 GMT
```

Again, it's no surprise that the Ajax request is made every time the user opens the spreadsheet. The response does not have a header telling the browser to cache it. In my test, I wasn't modifying the spreadsheet, so this response was identical every time I opened my spreadsheet. In fact, 8 of the 10 requests were identical, so it raises the question of whether they could have been cached.

Just as in the Yahoo! Mail example, caching the spreadsheet is not as easy as adding a far future `Expires` header. If the user modifies the spreadsheet, we need to ensure that cached requests affected by the changes aren't reused. Again, a simple solution is to use the query string. The Google Spreadsheets backend could save a timestamp representing when the last modifications were made, and embed this in the query string of the Ajax requests:

```
/ar?id=[snip...]&srow=0&erow=100&t=1177458941
```

Although the Ajax requests aren't cacheable, other performance guidelines are implemented successfully. The response is gzipped (Rule 4). As with most Google sites, domain lookups are minimized (Rule 9). The scripts are minified (Rule 10). It doesn't use redirects (Rule 11). And the ETags are removed (Rule 13).

> Make sure your Ajax requests follow the performance guidelines, especially having a far future Expires header.

What follows is an examination of 10 top U.S. web sites using the rules and tools described in this book. This analysis gives examples of how to identify performance improvements in real-world web sites. My hope is that after walking through these examples you will look at web sites with the critical eye of a performance advocate.

Page Weight, Response Time, YSlow Grade

Table 15-1 shows the page weight, response time, and YSlow grade for the home pages of 10 top U.S. web sites as measured in early 2007. YSlow is a performance tool developed at Yahoo! that produces a single score (A is best, F is worst) for how well a page satisfies the performance rules described in this book. See the upcoming section "How the Tests Were Done" for more information.

Table 15-1. Performance summary of 10 top U.S. web sites

	Page weight	Response time	YSlow grade
Amazon	405K	15.9 sec	D
AOL	182K	11.5 sec	F
CNN	502K	22.4 sec	F
eBay	275K	9.6 sec	C
Google	18K	1.7 sec	A
MSN	221K	9.3 sec	F
MySpace	205K	7.8 sec	D
Wikipedia	106K	6.2 sec	C
Yahoo!	178K	5.9 sec	A
YouTube	139K	9.6 sec	D

Not surprisingly, page weight and response time are strongly correlated, with a correlation coefficient of 0.94, as shown in Figure 15-1. This makes sense—adding more components or larger components to the page makes it slower. Plotting page weight and response time throughout the development process is a worthwhile analysis for any web page undergoing performance improvements.

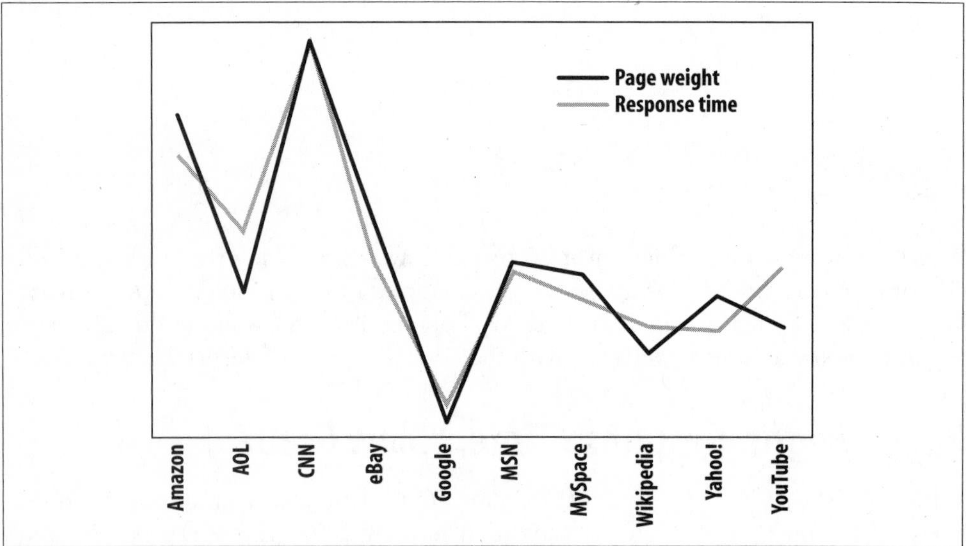

Figure 15-1. Page weight and response time are correlated

YSlow grades are a strong indicator of the response time of a page, as shown in Figure 15-2. A high (good) YSlow grade indicates a well-built page that is fast and lean. A page with a low (bad) YSlow grade is probably going to be slow and heavier. Since the YSlow grade is inversely related to response time and page weight, the inverse YSlow grade is plotted in Figure 15-2. YSlow grades are typically indicated as A, B, C, D, or F, but behind the letter grade is a numeric score on the scale 0–100.

Yahoo! doesn't quite follow the curve. It has the second-best YSlow grade (its score is A, at 95, which is slightly lower than Google's A, a perfect 100) and response time, even though it's the fourth-heaviest page. The Yahoo! home page team is a long-time consumer of these performance best practices, and therefore scores well in YSlow and is able to squeeze more speed out of their page. Amazon's YSlow grade also doesn't reflect the page weight and response time. The main reason for this is the large number of images in their page (approximately 74 images). YSlow doesn't subtract points for images, so the Amazon page scores well, but performs slowly.

In general, we see that following these best practices results in a faster page. The correlation coefficient for inverse YSlow grade and response time is 0.76, indicating a strong correlation. This has been my experience in working with product teams at Yahoo!. As pages are changed to adopt one rule after another, their response times

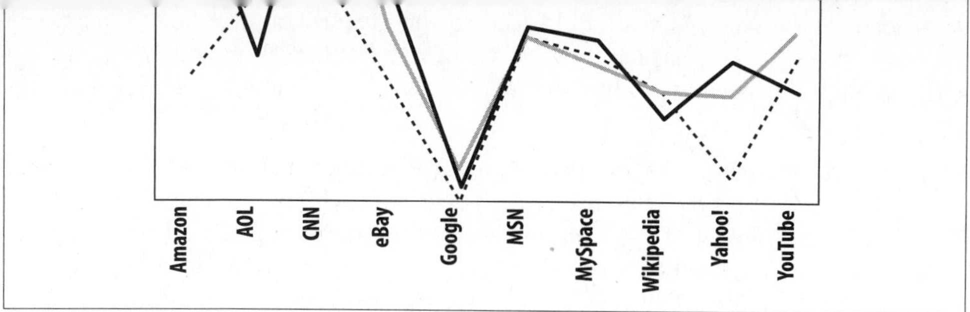

Figure 15-2. YSlow grade is inversely correlated to page weight and response time

get faster and faster. In the next section, "How the Tests Were Done," I review the tools and measurements used in this analysis. After that, we'll jump into the performance analysis of these 10 top web sites.

How the Tests Were Done

Reviewing these 10 top web sites illustrates how performance best practices are followed in real world pages. A problem in doing an analysis of this type is that the subject of the analysis is a moving target—these web sites are constantly changing. For example, during my analysis one web site switched from IIS to Apache. It's possible, and likely, that the page I analyzed is not the one you'll see if you visit that web site today. Ideally, the page you find will implement the suggestions and other best practices highlighted here, and will perform well and load quickly.

The charts of HTTP requests were generated by IBM Page Detailer (*http://alphaworks.ibm.com/tech/pagedetailer*). This is my preferred packet sniffer. It works across all HTTP clients. I like the way IBM Page Detailer indicates how the HTTP requests are associated to the corresponding HTML document. The HTTP chart makes it easy to identify bottlenecks in component downloads. The bars are color-coded to indicate the type of component being downloaded.

The response times were measured using Gomez's web monitoring services (*http://www.gomez.com*). The *response time* is defined as the time from when the request is initiated to when the page's `onload` event fires. Each URL was measured thousands of times over low broadband (56K–512K); the average value is what is shown here.

I used Firebug (*http://www.getfirebug.com*) to analyze the JavaScript and CSS in the various pages. Firebug is a critical tool for any frontend engineer. Its strongest feature is the ability to debug JavaScript code, but that's just a fraction of what it can do. Firebug also provides functionality to inspect the DOM, tweak CSS, execute JavaScript, and explore the page's HTML.

The main tool used to analyze the performance of these pages was YSlow (*http://developer.yahoo.com/yslow*). I built YSlow for Yahoo! development teams to help them identify the changes that could lead to the greatest improvements in performance. Joe Hewitt, Firebug's author, provided support for the integration of YSlow with Firebug. This is an ideal combination since frontend engineers already use Firebug during development.

YSlow crawls the page's DOM to find all the components in the page. It uses `XMLHttpRequest` to find the response time and size of each component, as well as the HTTP response headers. This, along with other information gathered from parsing the page's HTML is used to score each rule, as shown in Figure 15-3. The overall YSlow grade is a weighted average of each rule's score. YSlow provides other tools as well, including a summary of the page's components and an analysis of all the JavaScript in the page using JSLint (*http://jslint.com*).

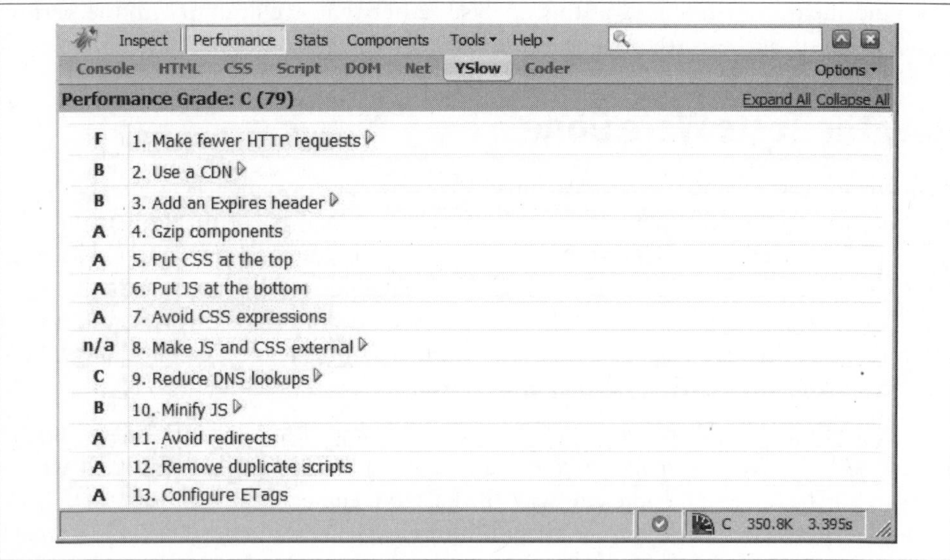

Figure 15-3. YSlow

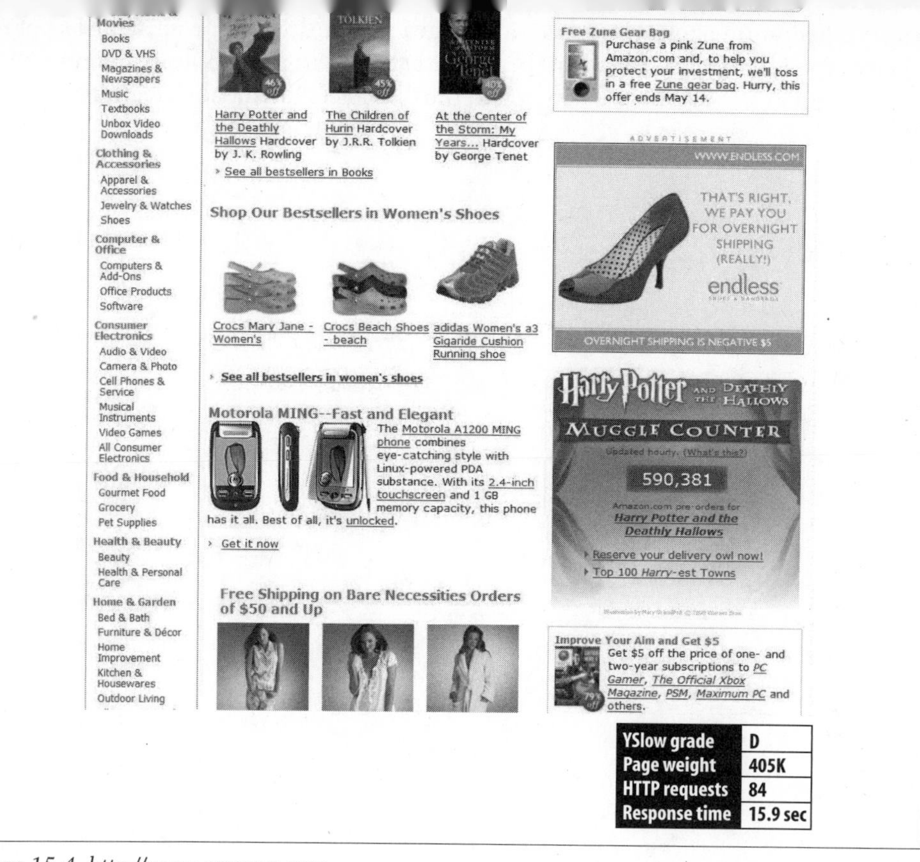

YSlow grade	D
Page weight	405K
HTTP requests	84
Response time	15.9 sec

Figure 15-4. http://www.amazon.com

Amazon (*http://www.amazon.com*) is a relatively heavy page with a total page weight of 405K and 84 HTTP requests. Given the size and number of components in the page, the biggest performance improvement for Amazon would be to add a far future `Expires` header to their components (Rule 3). Only 3 out of 84 components have an `Expires` header. They use only one stylesheet and three scripts. The scripts are loaded one after the other, so it would be a simple improvement to combine them into a single HTTP request. The stylesheet and scripts should be gzipped. The three scripts are minified to a large degree, but further savings could be gained by removing all comments and extraneous carriage returns.

Even with the performance improvements identified by YSlow, the sheer number of images in the page (74) is a challenge. Nineteen of these images are used as backgrounds in CSS rules. Converting them into CSS sprites would reduce the total HTTP requests from 84 to 66.

Looking at the subset of HTTP requests shown in the waterfall chart in Figure 15-5, we see that because these images are all requested from the same hostname, only two images are downloaded in parallel, increasing the total page load time. Splitting this large number of images across two hostnames would double the amount of parallel downloads, significantly reducing the end user response time. Two is the number of hostnames recommended in Chapter 6 in the "Parallel Downloads" section.

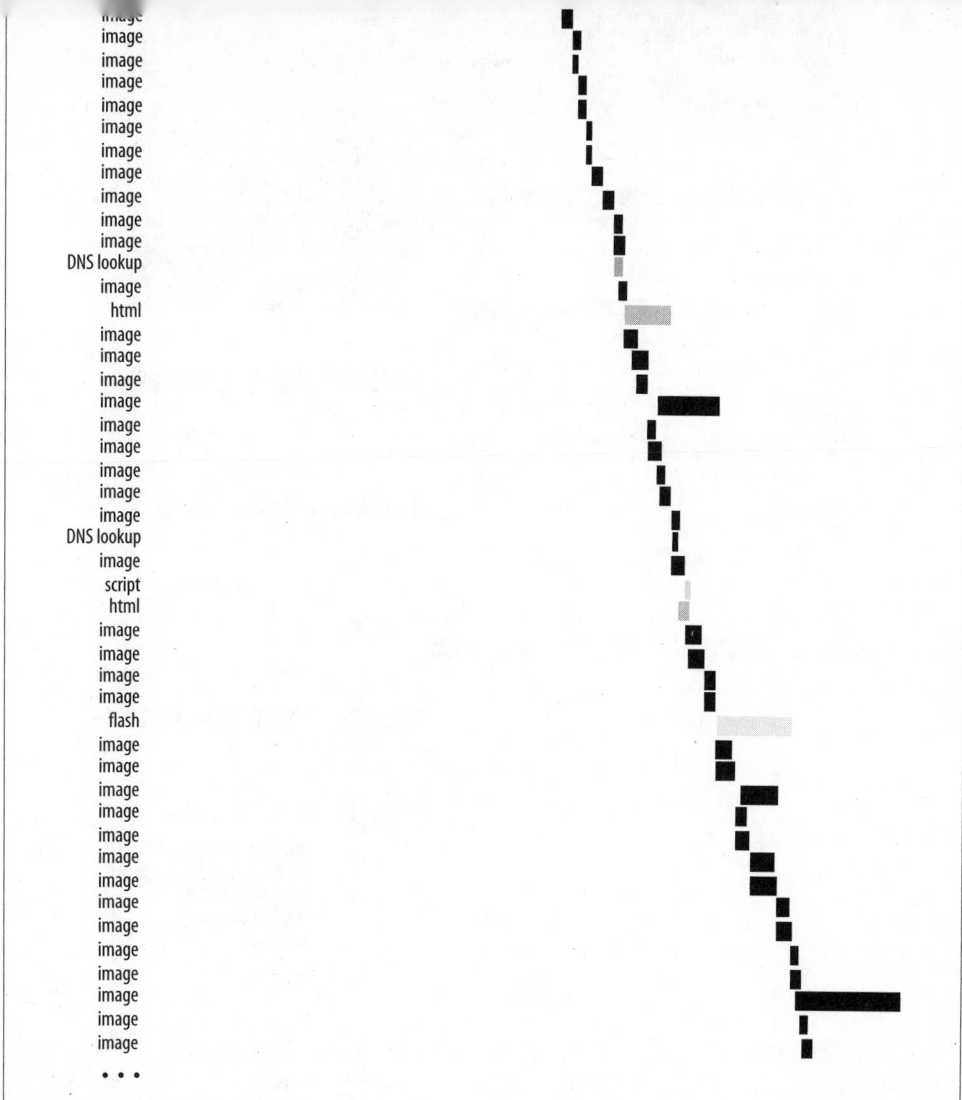

Figure 15-5. Amazon HTTP requests

AOL

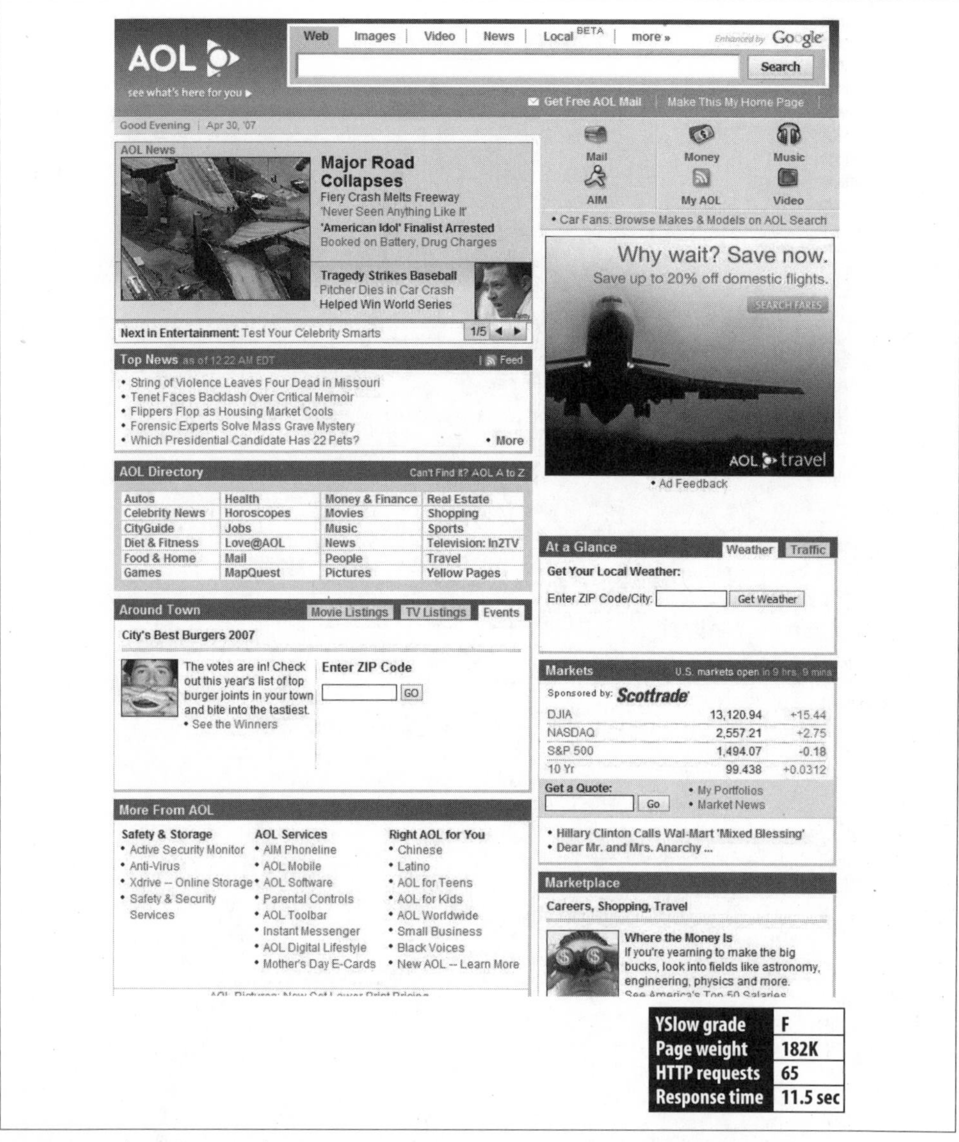

Figure 15-6. http://www.aol.com

The HTTP requests for AOL (*http://www.aol.com*) show a high degree of parallelization of downloads in the first half, but in the second half, the HTTP requests are made sequentially (see Figure 15-7). In turn, the page load time is increased. There are two interesting implementation details here: downgrading to HTTP/1.0 and multiple scripts.

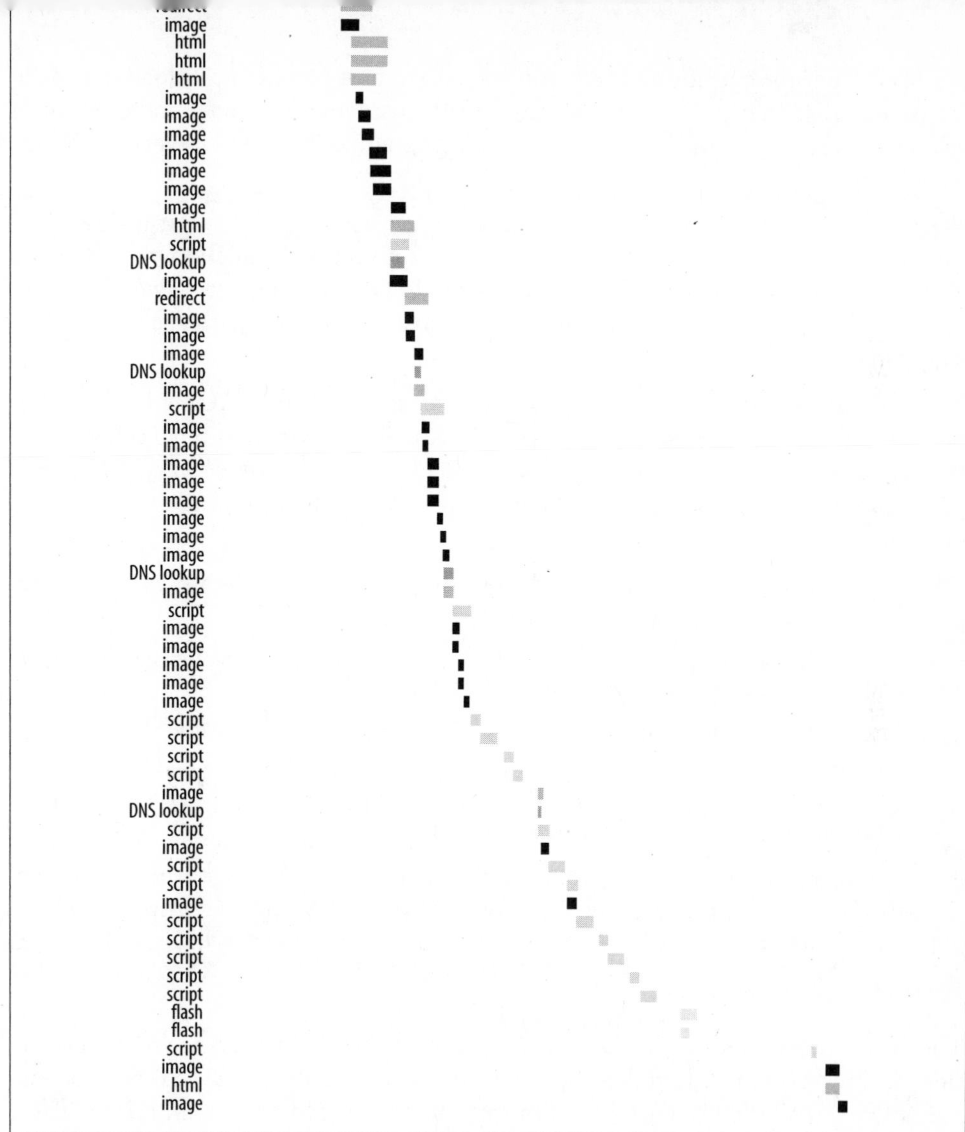

Figure 15-7. AOL HTTP requests

In the first half, where there is greater parallelization, the responses have been downgraded from HTTP/1.1 to HTTP/1.0. I discovered this by looking at the HTTP headers where the request method specifies `HTTP/1.1`, whereas the response states `HTTP/1.0`.

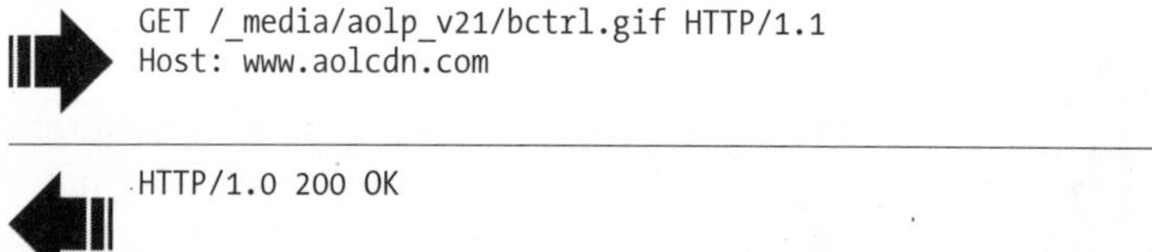

GET /_media/aolp_v21/bctrl.gif HTTP/1.1
Host: www.aolcdn.com
HTTP/1.0 200 OK

For HTTP/1.0, the specification recommends up to four parallel downloads per hostname, versus HTTP/1.1's guideline of two per hostname. Greater parallelization is achieved as a result of the web server downgrading the HTTP version in the response.

Typically, I've seen this result from outdated server configurations, but it's also possible that it's done intentionally to increase the amount of parallel downloading. At Yahoo!, we tested this, but determined that HTTP/1.1 had better overall performance because it supports persistent connections by default (see the section "Keep-Alive" in Chapter B).

There are no parallel downloads in much of the second half of AOL's HTTP traffic because most of these requests are scripts. As described in Chapter 6, all other downloading is blocked while the browser downloads external scripts. This results in a small number of requests spreading out over a longer time period than if they were done in parallel.

These scripts appear to be used for ads, but the insertion of the scripts seems inefficient. The scripts come in pairs. The first script contains:

```
document.write('<script type="text/javascript" src="http://twx.doubleclick.net/adj/
TW.AOLCom/Site_WS[snip...]script>\n');
```

This causes the second script to be downloaded from *http://twx.doubleclick.net*. It contains the content of the ad:

```
document.write('<!-- Template Id = 4140 Template Name = AOL - Text - WS Portal ATF DR
2-line (291x30) -->\n<B>Free Credit Score</B>[snip...]');
```

There are 6 ads done this way, totaling 12 external scripts that have to be downloaded. If each ad could be called and downloaded using just one script per ad, six HTTP requests could be eliminated. These additional requests have a significant impact on the page load time because they're scripts that block all other downloads.

The other areas for greatest improvement are:

Rule 3: Add an Expires Header
: More than 30 images aren't cached because they don't have an `Expires` header.

"204 No Content" status code. This status code is ideal for beacons because it does not contain an entity body, making the responses smaller.

CNN

Figure 15-8. http://www.cnn.com

CNN (*http://www.cnn.com*) is the heaviest of the 10 top web sites in both total page weight (502K) and number of HTTP requests (198!). The main reason for this is the use of images to display text. For example, the image *http://i.a.cnn.net/cnn/element/img/1.5/main/tabs/topstories.gif* is the text "Top Stories," as shown in Figure 15-9.

TOP STORIES

Figure 15-9. Text rendered in an image

Similarly, there are 16 images used for CSS backgrounds. If these were combined into a few CSS sprites, as described in Chapter 1, 10 or more HTTP requests would be eliminated. Combining the 10 separate JavaScript files together would eliminate another 9 HTTP requests.

Further, more than 140 of the components in the page do not have an `Expires` header and thus are not cached by the browser (Rule 3). None of the stylesheets or scripts is gzipped (Rule 4) and most of the scripts aren't minified (Rule 10). The stylesheets add up to 87K and the scripts are 114K, so gzipping and minifying would significantly reduce the total page weight. Over 180 of the components have the default ETag from Apache. As described in Chapter 13, this means that it's unlikely the more efficient 304 status code can be used when conditional GET requests are made. This is especially bad in this case because most components must be validated since they don't have a future `Expires` header.

eBay

Figure 15-10. http://www.ebay.com

The YSlow grade for eBay (*http://www.ebay.com*) is very close to a B. With a little bit of work it would perform well. The main problems are with Rules 1, 3, 9, and 13.

Rule 3: Add an Expires Header

One script and one stylesheet have an `Expires` header that is only nine hours in the future. According to the `Last-Modified` date, the stylesheet hasn't been modified in 3 days, and the script in 24 days. These are likely assets that change over time, but given the number of users of the site, it would be better to use a far future `Expires` header to make these files cacheable. Additionally, there are five IFrames without an `Expires` header. These are used to insert ad images, some of which don't have an `Expires` header as well.

Rule 9: Reduce DNS Lookups

Nine different domains are used in the eBay page. Typically, a domain count this high includes several domains from third-party advertisers, but in this case, there are seven domains related to eBay, and only two used by third-party advertisers.

Rule 13: ETags—Configure ETags

Fifty-two components are served from IIS using the default ETag. As explained in Chapter 13, this causes components to be downloaded much more frequently than necessary. This is exacerbated by the fact that these components have an expiration date that is at most 45 days in the future. As the components become stale and the conditional GET request is made, the ETag is likely to spoil the chances of getting a fast "304 Not Modified" response, and instead end up sending back the entire component even though it already resides on the user's disk.

The use of IFrames to serve ads is worth discussing. IFrames achieve a clear separation between ads and the actual web page, allowing those teams and systems to work independently. The downside is that each IFrame is an additional HTTP request that typically (as in this case) is not cached.

Using IFrames to serve ads is further justified because ads often contain their own JavaScript code. If the ad content is coming from a third party and includes JavaScript, placing it in an IFrame sandboxes the JavaScript code, resulting in greater security (the third party's JavaScript code cannot access the web page's namespace). However, in eBay's page, the ads served in IFrames include no JavaScript. Furthermore, only one contains third-party content. Inserting the ads during HTML page generation would eliminate these five HTTP requests for IFrames.

An additional improvement would be to split the bulk of the images across two hostnames. Thirty-six of the 41 images come from *http://pics.ebaystatic.com*. In HTTP/1.1, only two components per hostname are downloaded in parallel (see Chapter 6). This has a negative effect on the degree of HTTP request parallelization (see Figure 15-11).

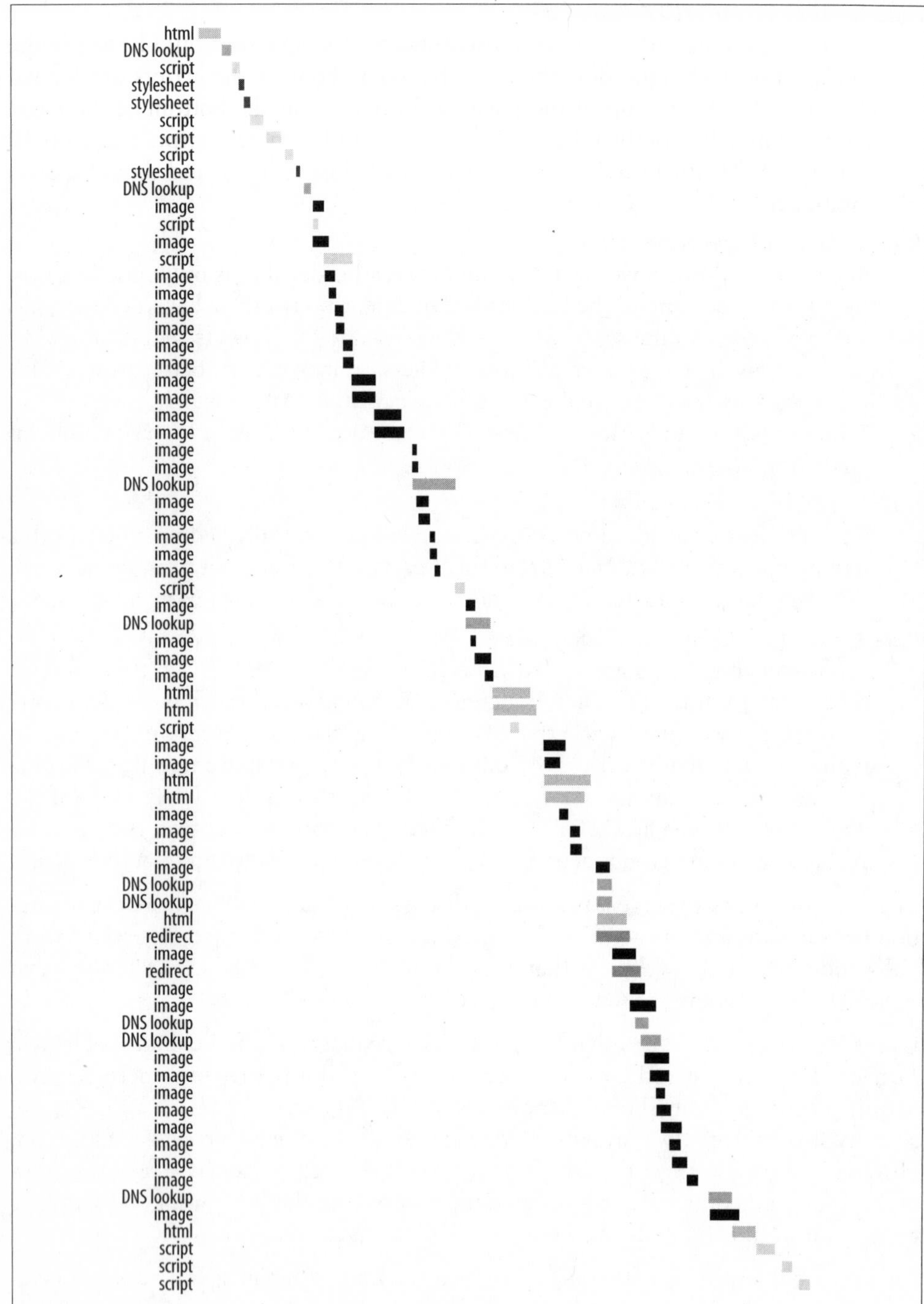

Figure 15-11. eBay HTTP requests

A nice performance trait is that three of the scripts are downloaded at the bottom of the page. These scripts are related to the user's eBay "Favorites" and are probably not required for rendering the page. eBay has followed the recommended practice here of loading scripts at the bottom, which Chapter 6 explained as valuable because it doesn't block downloading and rendering.

Google

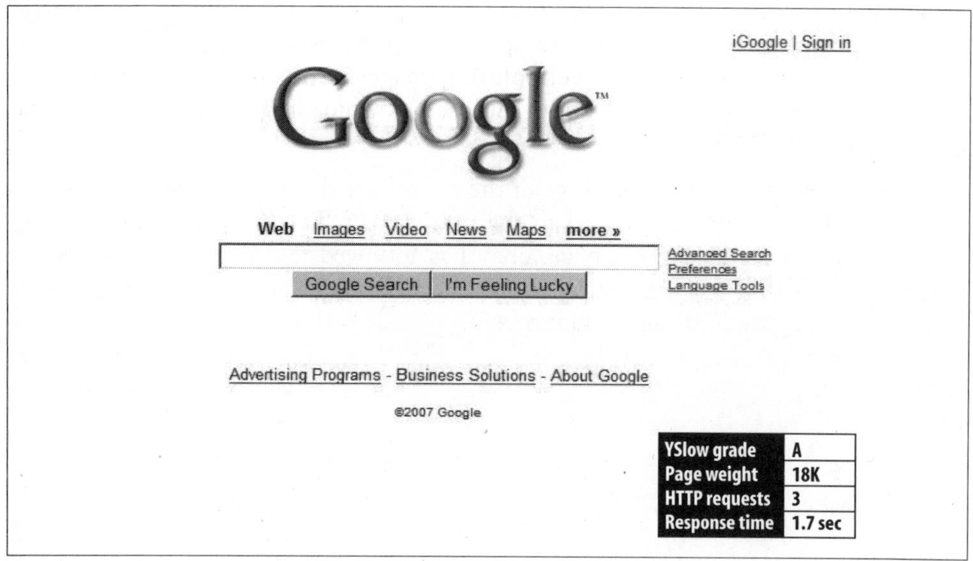

Figure 15-12. http://www.google.com

Google is known for its simple and fast page design. Its home page, *http://www.google.com*, is just 18K in total page size and issues just 3 HTTP requests (the HTML document and 2 images). However, even in this simple page there are several performance optimizations worth noting.

The Google page is just three HTTP requests, but Figure 15-13 shows five HTTP requests.

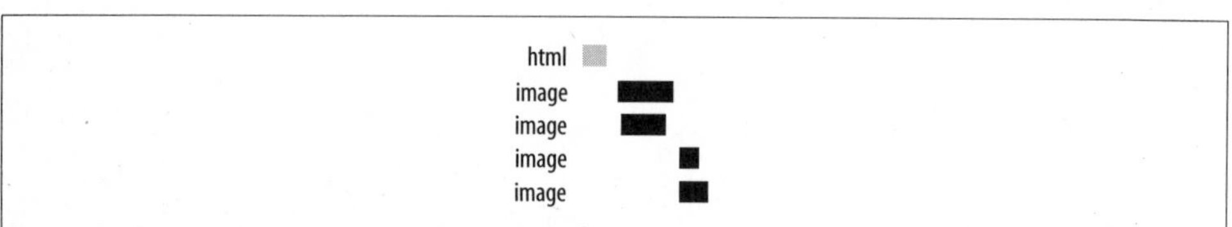

Figure 15-13. Google HTTP requests

The two extra requests aren't really part of the page. One is *http://www.google.com/favicon.ico* (see Figure 15-14). Favicons are used to associate a visual image with a URL. They are displayed next to the URL at the top of the browser, next to each URL in the list of Bookmarks or Favorites, and in tabs (for tab-enabled browsers). Browsers fetch them the first time a web site is loaded. If a web site doesn't have a favicon, a default icon is used.

```
onload="sf();if(document.images){new Image().src='/images/nav_logo3.png'}"
```

The `sf()` function call sets the input focus to the search field. The second statement creates an image object using `new Image()`. The image object's `src` attribute is set to `/images/nav_logo3.png`. This is a typical way to load images dynamically, except for one thing: the new image isn't assigned to a variable. There is no easy way for the page to access this image later. That's OK, though, because this page has no intention of using the image. The *nav_logo3.png* image is downloaded in anticipation of future pages the user is expected to visit. Notice how this CSS sprite has the next and previous arrows used to page through the search results. It also contains images used in other pages, such as a checkout button and shopping cart.

Figure 15-15. http://www.google.com/images/nav_logo3.png

This is called *preloading*. In situations where the next page the user will visit is highly predictable, components needed by that subsequent page are downloaded in the background. In the Google page, however, there is one problem: *nav_logo3.png* isn't used by any subsequent pages. After submitting a search from *http://www.google.com*, the user goes to *http://www.google.com/search*. The search results page loads *http://www.google.com/images/nav_logo.png* (no "3" after "logo"). As shown in Figure 15-16, *nav_logo.png* is similar to *nav_logo3.png*. It's also a CSS sprite.

Figure 15-16. http://www.google.com/images/nav_logo.png

Why did the Google home page preload *nav_logo3.png* if it's not used on the search results page? It's possible it's preloaded for other Google sites, but I visited *http://froogle.google.com*, *http://catalogs.google.com*, *http://books.google.com*, and several others. None of them used *nav_logo3.png*. Perhaps this is left over from a previous design and just hasn't been cleaned up. It could also be a foreshadowing of a future site integration strategy (hence the "3"). Despite this apparently wasteful download on the Google home page, don't be dissuaded. Preloading is a good strategy for improving the page load times of secondary pages on your site.

Another interesting performance optimization in the Google home page is the use of the `SCRIPT DEFER` attribute. In Chapter 6, I describe how the `DEFER` attribute doesn't completely resolve the negative performance impacts that scripts have when they block downloads and rendering. However, that was in regard to external scripts; in this case, the script is inlined:

```
<script type="text/javascript" defer><!--
function qs(el){...
function togDisp(e){...
function stopB(e){...
document.onclick=function(event){...
//-->
</script>
```

Using the `DEFER` attribute avoids possible rendering delays by telling the browser to continue rendering and execute the JavaScript later, but I've never seen it used for inline scripts. The justification for using it with an inline script may be that parsing and executing the JavaScript code could delay rendering the page. In this case, however, a problem is that after this `SCRIPT` block, there is a link that relies on the `togDisp` function to display a pop-up `DIV` of "more" links:

```
<a href="/intl/en/options/" onclick="this.blur();return togDisp(event)">more</a>
```

If using the `DEFER` attribute allowed the page to render without executing the `togDisp` function definition, a race condition would be created. If the "more" link is rendered and the user clicks on it before the JavaScript is executed, an error would occur. The use of `DEFER` on inline scripts is an area for further investigation.

These suggestions, however, are far beyond the typical performance improvements needed on most sites. The Google page scores a perfect 100 in YSlow—it is one of the fastest pages on the Internet.

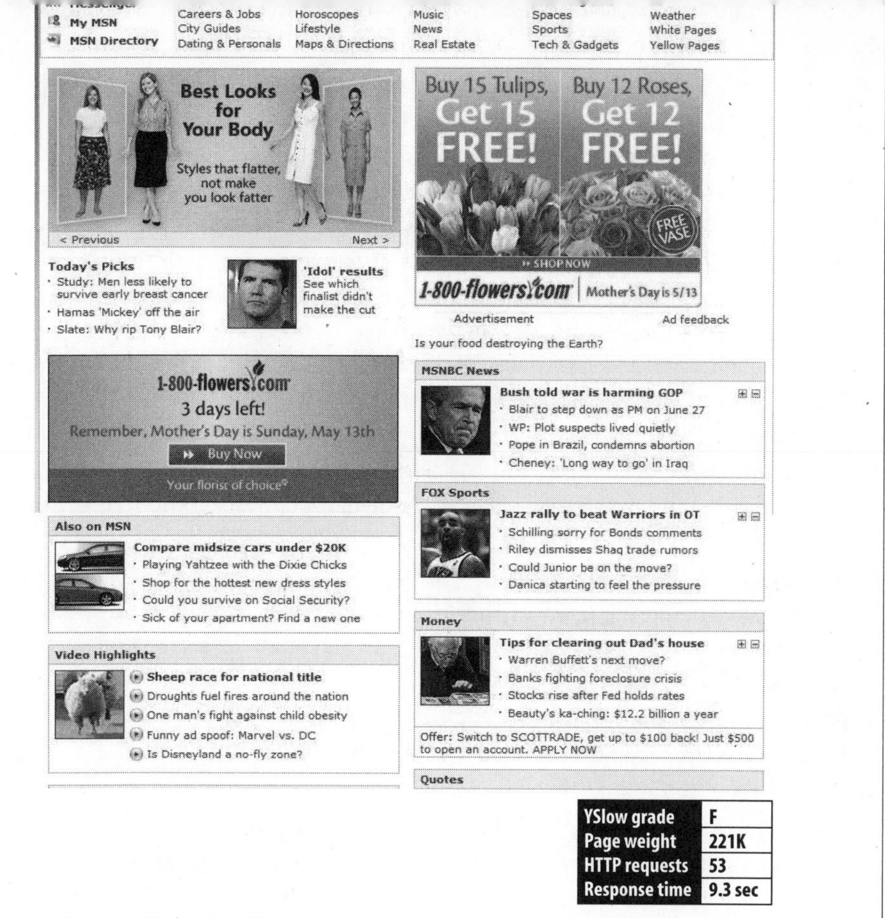

Figure 15-17. http://www.msn.com

The MSN home page (*http://www.msn.com*), ranks in the middle among the sites examined in this chapter when it comes to total size and number of HTTP requests. It fails to meet some basic performance guidelines, due especially to the way ads are inserted. However, it has several positive performance traits not seen in any of the other web sites analyzed here. Let's start by looking at how MSN does ads, because this will come up in several of the following recommendations.

MSN uses IFrames to insert five ads into the page. As discussed earlier, with regard to eBay, using IFrames is an easy way to remove dependencies between the ads system and the HTML page generation system. However, each IFrame results in an additional HTTP request. In the case of MSN, each IFrame's `SRC` attribute is set to `about:blank`, which doesn't generate any HTTP traffic. However, each IFrame contains an external script that inserts an ad into the page using JavaScript and `document.write`. Integrating the ad system and the HTML page generation system would preclude the need for these five HTTP requests. Instead of requesting a script that contains multiple `document.write` statements, that JavaScript could be inlined in the HTML document.

Rule 1: Make Fewer HTTP Requests
: The MSN home page has four scripts (other than the scripts used for ads), three of which are loaded very close together and could be combined. It also has over 10 CSS background images. These could be combined using CSS sprites.

Rule 3: Add an Expires Header
: One script is not cacheable because its expiration date is set in the past. The five scripts used to insert ads also have an expiration date in the past, and so they aren't cacheable. It's likely the JavaScript couldn't be cached, but if the ads were inserted into the HTML page itself, these five external script files wouldn't be required.

Rule 4: Gzip Components
: Two scripts and two stylesheets are not gzipped. Also, the five scripts used to serve ads are not gzipped.

Rule 9: Reduce DNS Lookups
: Twelve domains are used in the MSN home page. This is more than most web pages, but we'll discuss later how this is a benefit in increasing parallel downloads.

Rule 10: Minify JavaScript
: The five scripts used to serve ads are not minified.

Rule 13: ETags—Configure ETags
: Most of the components in the page have ETags that follow the default format for IIS. The same images downloaded from different servers have different ETags, meaning they will be downloaded more frequently than needed.

Several noteworthy performance optimizations exist in the MSN home page:

- It uses a CSS sprite (*http://stc.msn.com/br/hp/en-us/css/19/decoration/buttons.gif*), one of the few 10 top web sites to do so (the others are AOL and Yahoo!). This sprite is shown in Figure 15-18.

downloads, as shown in Figure 13-19. This is done in a very deliberate way—all CSS images are from a different hostname from the other images displayed in the page.

MSN clearly has people on its staff focused on some aspects of performance. However, integrating the ads with the HTML page and fixing a few web server configuration settings would greatly improve the performance of their page.

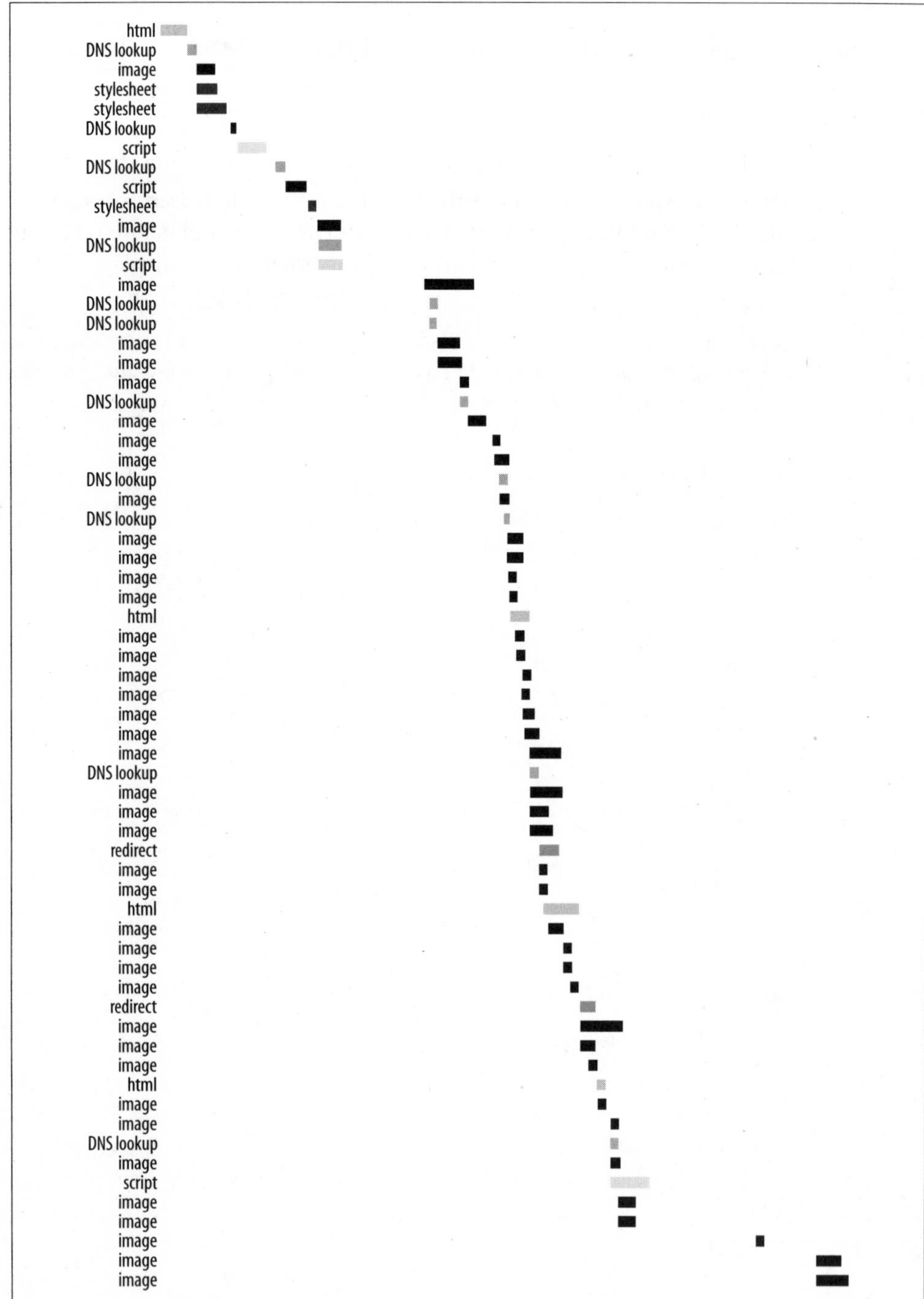

Figure 15-19. MSN HTTP requests

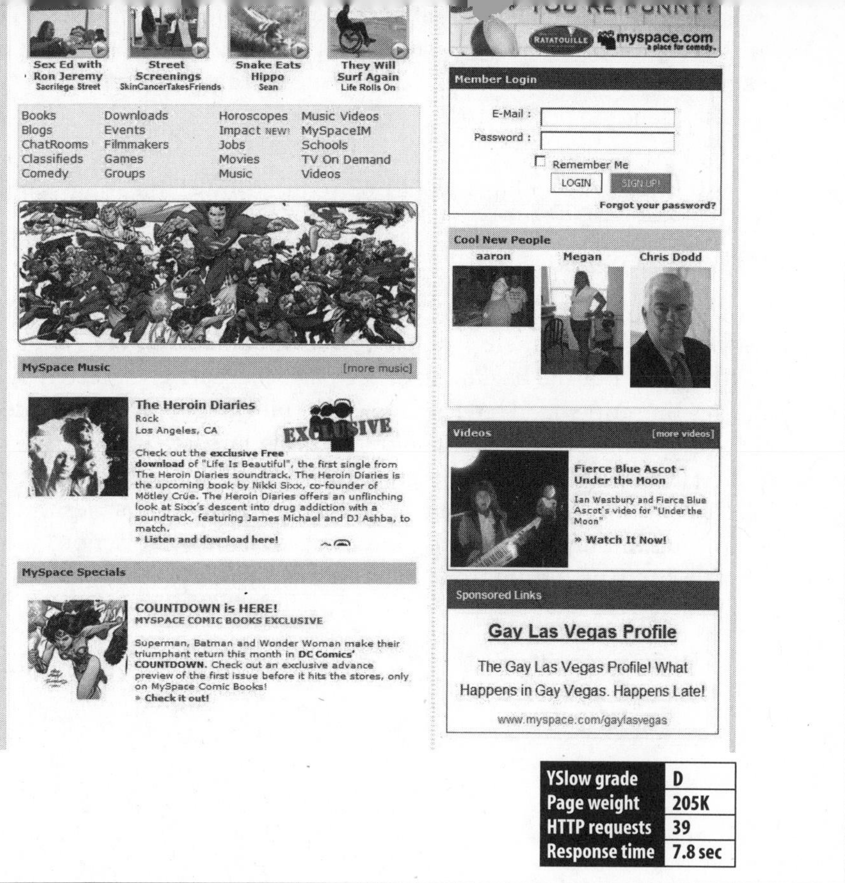

Figure 15-20. http://www.myspace.com

It's a challenge for web sites geared toward user-generated content to achieve fast performance—the content is varied and changes frequently. Nevertheless, there are some simple changes that would improve the response time of MySpace (*http://www.myspace.com*).

Rule 1: Make Fewer HTTP Requests
: Combining scripts and stylesheets would reduce the number of HTTP requests. The page has six scripts, three of which are loaded close together at the top of the page and could easily be combined. The three stylesheets are also loaded close together at the top of the page, making it easy to combine them as well.

Rule 3: Add an Expires Header
: The MySpace page has over a dozen images with no `Expires` header. Some of the images in the page understandably wouldn't benefit from an `Expires` header because they rotate frequently, such as in the new videos and new people sections of the page. However, some of the images that are used on every page also do not have an `Expires` header.

Rule 9: Reduce DNS Lookups
: The impact of DNS lookups would be reduced by eliminating some of the 10 unique domains used in the page.

Rule 10: Minify JavaScript
: Four scripts, totaling over 20K, are not minified.

As shown in Figure 15-21, there's a high degree of parallelized HTTP requests in the middle of the page, but the beginning of the page is negatively affected by the blocking behavior of scripts and stylesheets (this blocking behavior is described in Chapter 6). Combining these files would lessen the impact. The effect is worse here because the HTTP requests were measured in Firefox. In addition to scripts blocking parallel downloads (in both Firefox and Internet Explorer), stylesheets also block parallel downloads (only in Firefox). Nevertheless, combining scripts and doing the same for stylesheets would improve the performance for both Firefox and Internet Explorer.

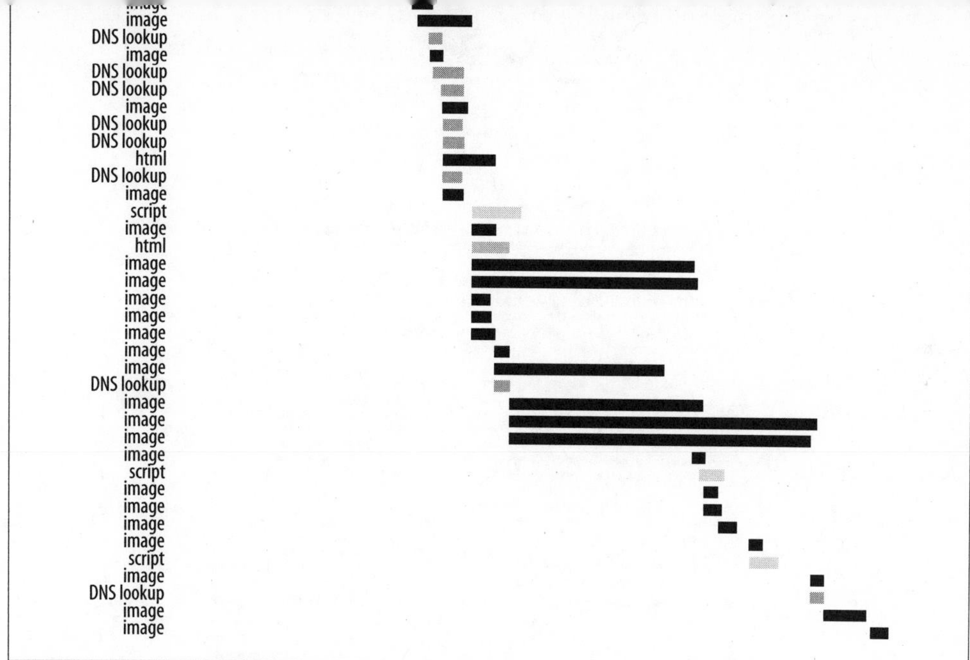

Figure 15-21. MySpace HTTP requests

Wikipedia

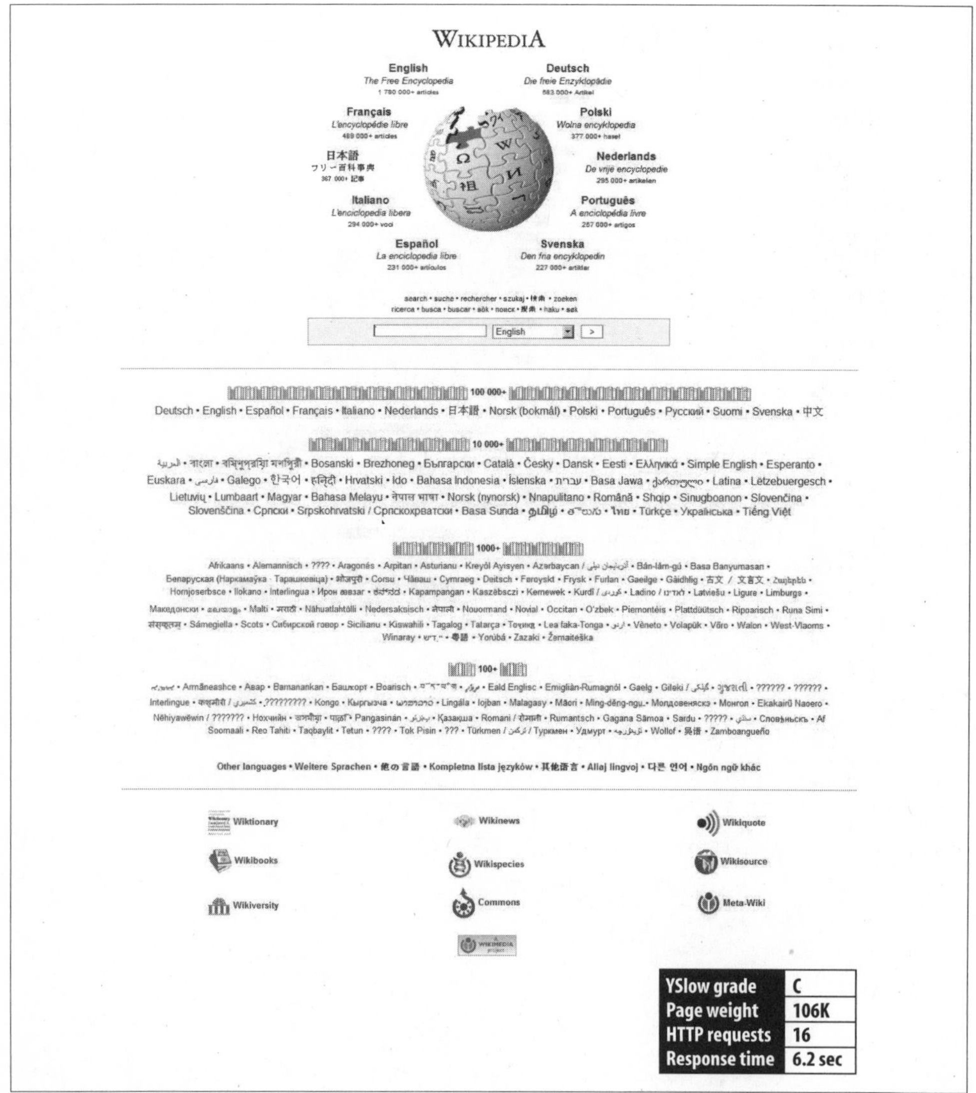

Figure 15-22. http://www.wikipedia.org

The Wikipedia page is relatively small and fast. It would be faster if the 10 images used as navigation icons at the bottom of the page were converted to a CSS sprite. Further, there are two stylesheets that should be combined. These simple improvements would reduce the page's HTTP requests from 16 to just 6: the HTML document, 1 stylesheet, 3 images, and 1 CSS sprite.

Most of Wikipedia's images are in PNG format. The PNG format is frequently chosen over GIF because of its smaller file size, as well as greater color depth and transparency options. It's likely that using the PNG format saved Wikipedia several kilobytes of data to download (it's not possible to convert their PNG images to GIF for comparison because of the loss of color depth). However, even after choosing the PNG format, further optimization can bring the file sizes down even more. For example, optimizing Wikipedia's 12 PNG images brought the total size from 33K down to 28K, a 15% savings. There are several PNG optimizers available—I used PngOptimizer (*http://psydk.org/PngOptimizer.php*). Adding a PNG optimization step to their development process would improve Wikipedia's performance.

Yahoo!

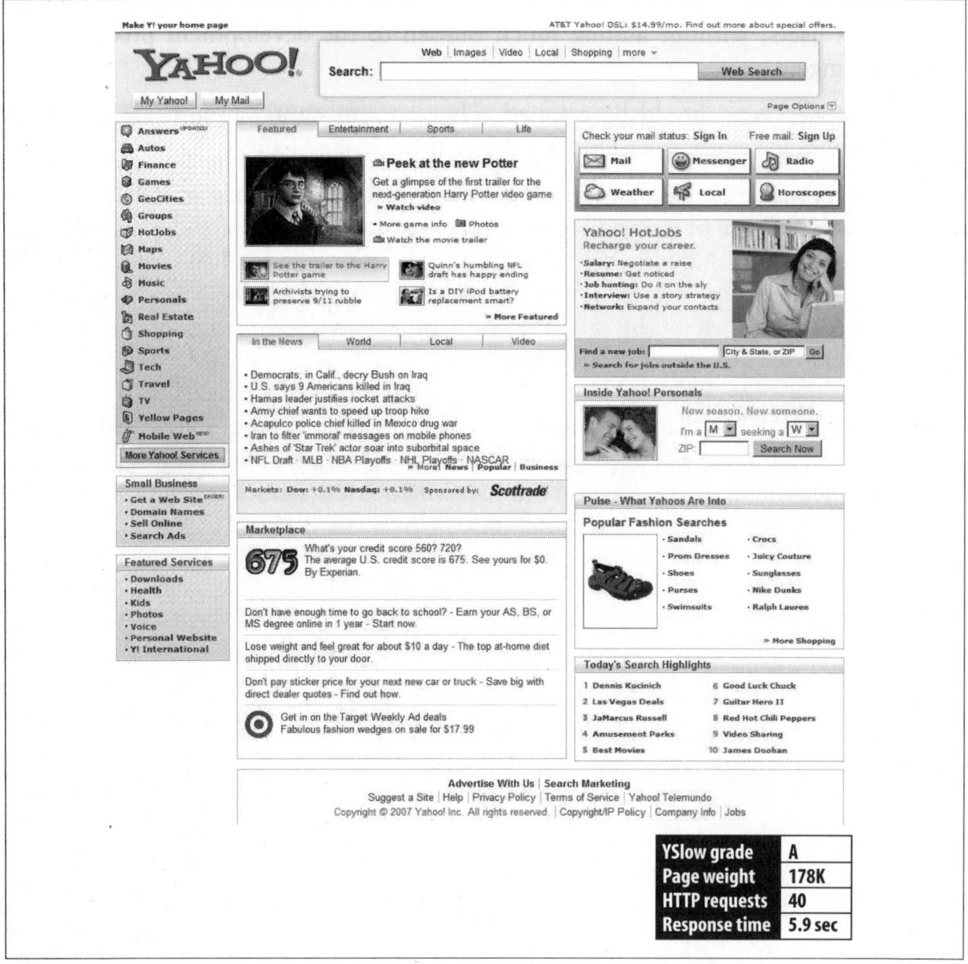

Figure 15-23. http://www.yahoo.com

Yahoo! (*http://www.yahoo.com*) is the fourth-heaviest page in total bytes among the ones examined in this chapter, but second in response time and YSlow grade. The Yahoo! home page team has been engaged with my performance team for years, and is constantly tracking and working to improve response times. As a result, their YSlow scores are high, and they are able to squeeze more speed out of their page.

Yahoo!'s home page has four CSS sprite images. It has been using sprites for years and was the first web site in which I encountered the use of sprites. One of these sprites is *icons_1.5.gif*. Looking at the list of components, we see that this image is in the HTML document, so presumably both had access to the same template variables. The *us.js2.yimg.com* hostname is used for all of the scripts, and *us.i1.yimg.com* is used solely for images and Flash. Most likely, the "JavaScript" hostname, *us.js2.yimg.com*, was accidentally used for this CSS background image.

This look at the use of hostnames reveals some nice performance optimizations in the Yahoo! home page. They have split their components across multiple hostnames, resulting in an increase in simultaneous downloads, as shown in Figure 15-24. Also, they have chosen the domain *yimg.com*, which is different from the page's hostname, *yahoo.com*. As a result, the HTTP requests to *yimg.com* will not be encumbered with any cookies that exist in the *yahoo.com* domain. When I'm logged in to my personal Yahoo! Account, my *yahoo.com* cookies are over 600 bytes, so this adds up to a savings of over 25K across all the HTTP requests in the page.

The names of two elements are intriguing: *onload_1.3.4.css* and *onload_1.4.8.js*. In Chapters 5 and 6 I talk about the negative impact that stylesheets and scripts have on performance (stylesheets block rendering in the page, and scripts block rendering and downloading for anything after them in the page). An optimization around this that I described in Chapter 8 is downloading these components after the page has finished loading, thus eliminating the negative blocking effect. This more extreme approach is applicable only when the stylesheet or script is not necessary for the rendering of the initial page. In the case of the Yahoo! home page, this stylesheet and script are most likely used for DHTML actions that occur *after* the page has loaded. For example, clicking on the "More Yahoo! Services" link displays a DHTML list of links to other Yahoo! properties. This functionality, which happens after the page has loaded, is contained in *onload_1.3.4.css*.

The main improvements that could be made to the Yahoo! home page, other than removing the duplicate CSS background image described earlier, would be to reduce the number of domains (seven) and combine the three scripts that are loaded as part of the page. Minifying the HTML document (as MSN does) would reduce it from 117K to 29K. Overall, the Yahoo! home page demonstrates several advanced performance optimizations and has a fast response time given the content and functionality included in the page.

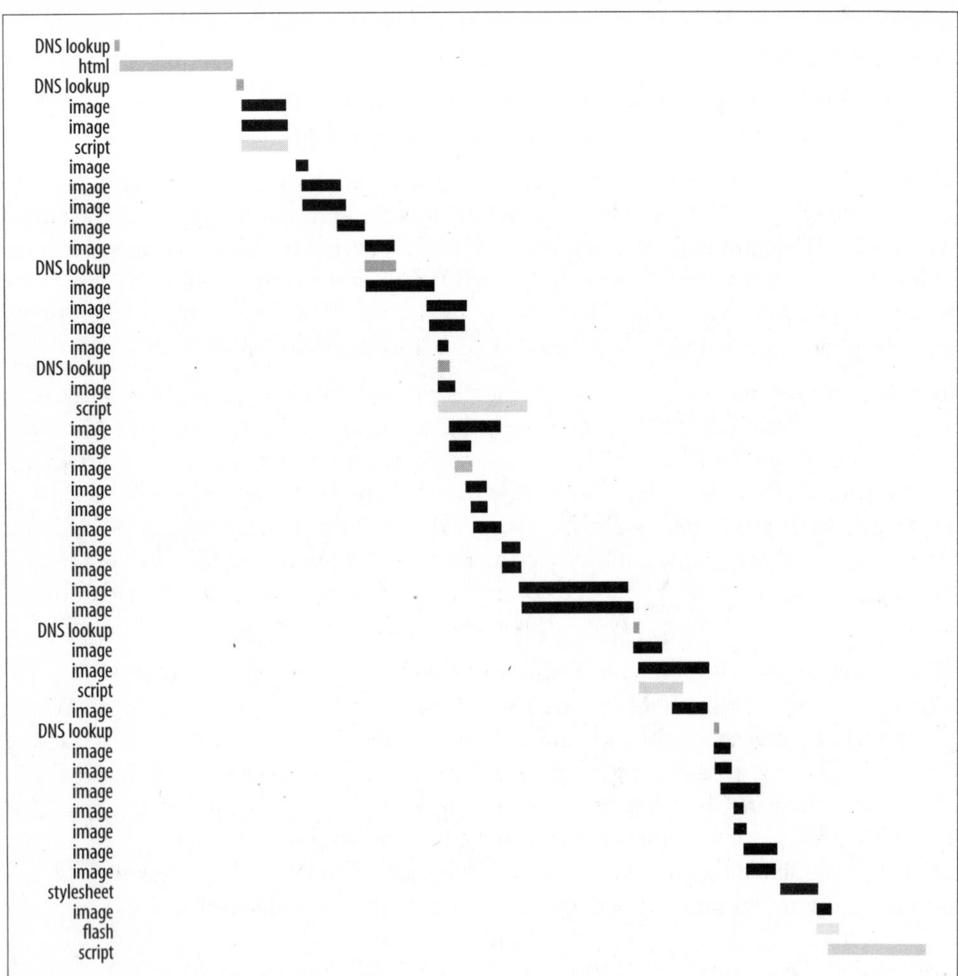

Figure 15-24. Yahoo! HTTP requests

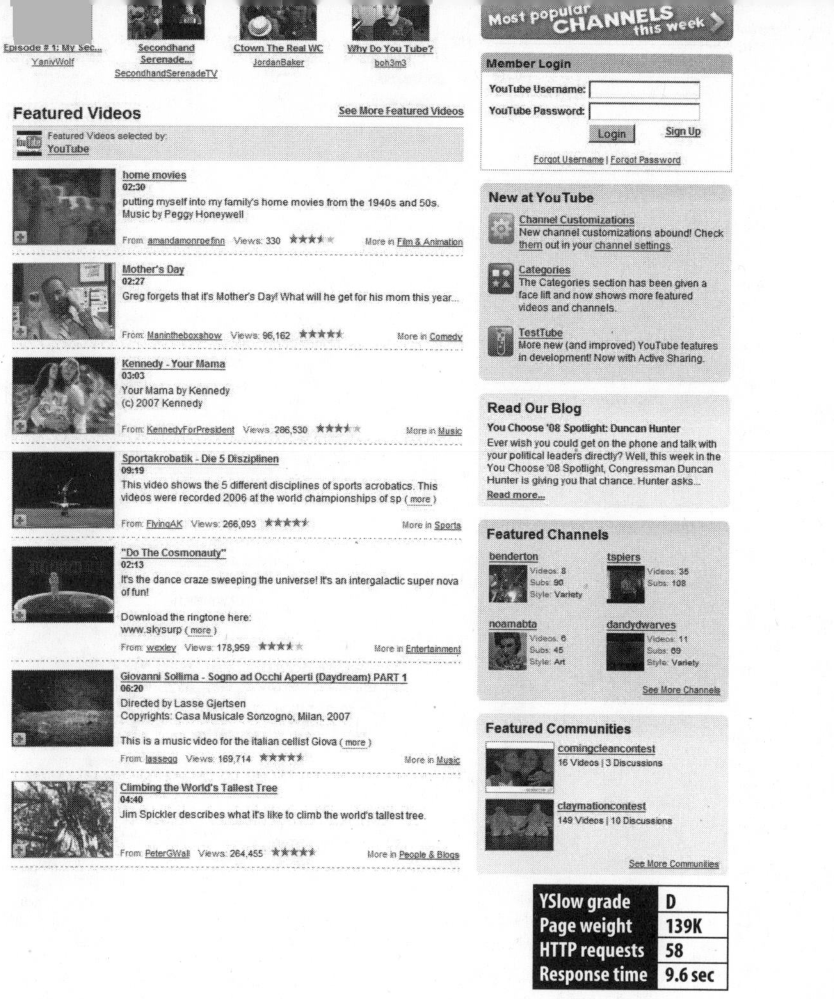

YSlow grade	D
Page weight	139K
HTTP requests	58
Response time	9.6 sec

Figure 15-25. http://www.youtube.com

YouTube's home page (*http://www.youtube.com*) isn't very heavy, but it has a low YSlow grade and ends up in the bottom half of response times. Figure 15-26 shows that there isn't very much parallelization at the beginning and end. Increasing the level of parallelization in these areas would make the greatest improvement to response times.

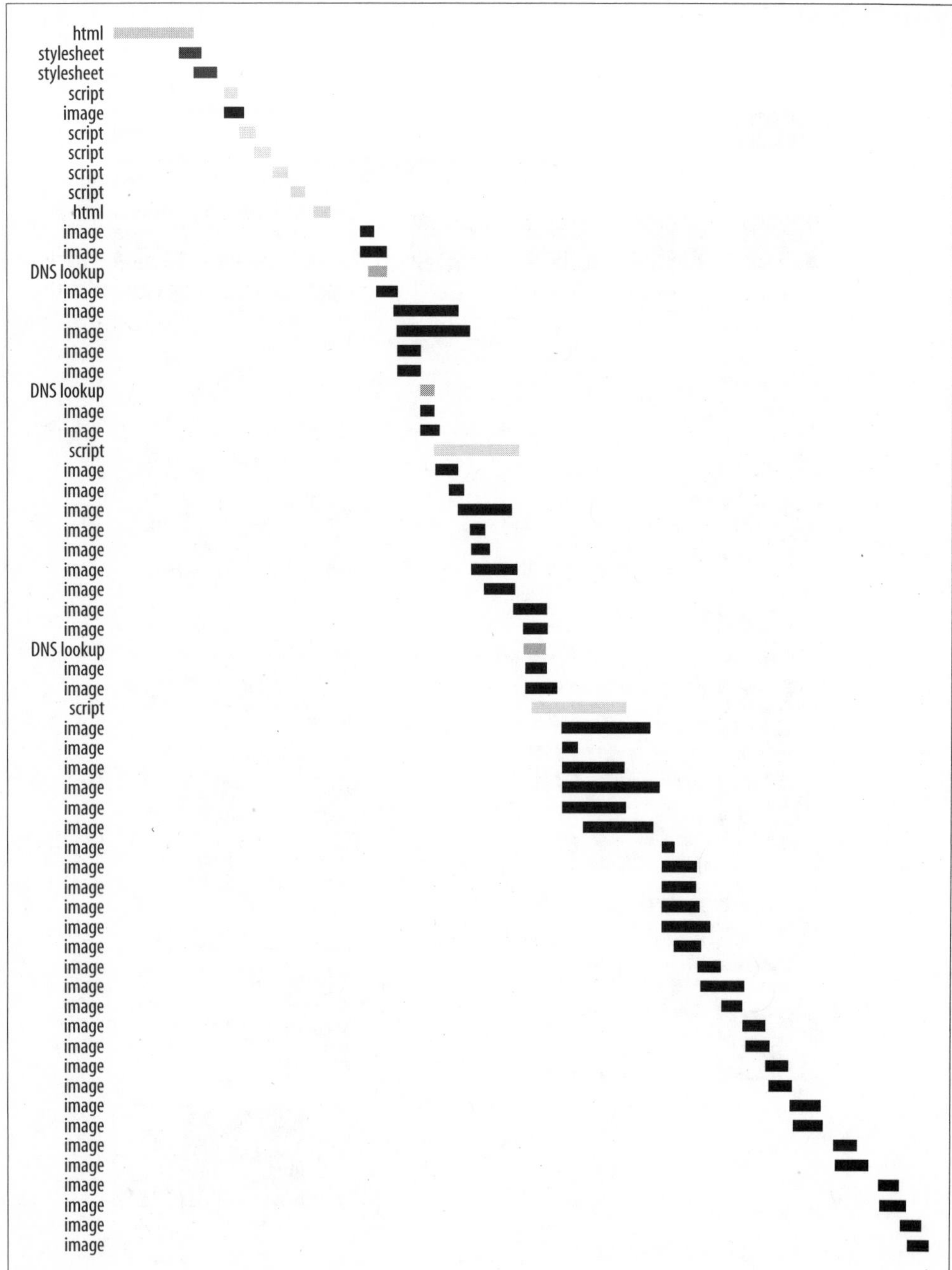

Figure 15-26. YouTube HTTP requests

from a single hostname (*img.youtube.com*). YouTube only uses four unique hostnames in their page. It would be worth the cost of an extra DNS lookup to split these 15 downloads across two hostnames and double the amount of simultaneous downloads.

Sadly, not a single component has a far future `Expires` header (Rule 3). Most of the components in the page are user-generated images that rotate frequently. Adding an `Expires` header to these might have little benefit, but the other components in the page don't change so often. Eleven of the components haven't changed in six months or more. Adding a far future `Expires` header to these components would improve the response times for subsequent page views.

YouTube uses the Apache web server, and their components still contain Etags, but YouTube has made the extra effort to modify the ETag syntax to improve their cacheability, as explained in Chapter 13..

Numbers

A

We'd like to hear your suggestions for improving our indexes. Send email to *index@oreilly.com*.

D

F

G

R

S

T

U

V

W

X

Y

web sites faster. He builds tools for performance analysis and evangelizes these best practices and tools across Yahoo!'s product teams.

Prior to Yahoo!, Steve worked at several small to mid-size startups, including two companies he cofounded: Helix Systems and CoolSync. He also worked at General Magic, WhoWhere?, and Lycos. In the early 1980s, Steve caught the Artificial Intelligence bug and worked at a few companies doing research on Machine Learning. He received a B.S. in Systems Engineering from the University of Virginia and an M.S. in Management Science and Engineering from Stanford University.

Steve's interests are varied. He sits on the board of Freehand Systems and Fremont Hills Country Club, and he teaches Sunday School. He's played basketball with several NBA and WNBA players, but has recently retired and switched to Ultimate Frisbee. He was a member of the Universal Studios Internet Task Force, has rebuilt a 90-year-old carriage house, and participated in setting a Guinness world record. He has a wonderful wife and three daughters.

Colophon

The animal on the cover of *High Performance Web Sites* is a greyhound.

The fastest dog in the world, a greyhound can reach speeds of up to 45 miles per hour, enabled by its streamlined, narrow body; large lungs, heart, and muscles; double suspension gallop (two periods of a gait when all four feet are off the ground); and the flexibility of its spine. Although greyhounds are incredibly fast, they are actually low-energy dogs and lack endurance, requiring less exercise time than most dogs. For this reason, they're often referred to as "45-mile-per-hour couch potatoes" because when not chasing smaller prey (such as rabbits and cats), they are content to spend their days sleeping.

Greyhounds are one of the oldest breeds of dogs, appearing in art and literature throughout history. In ancient Egypt, greyhounds were often mummified and buried with their owners, and hieroglyphics from 4000 B.C.E. show a dog closely resembling the modern greyhound. In Greek and Roman mythology, greyhounds were often depicted with gods and goddesses. Greyhounds appeared in the writings of Homer, Chaucer, Shakespeare, and Cervantes, and they are the only type of dog mentioned in the Bible. They've long been appreciated for their intelligence, graceful form, athleticism, and loyalty.

During the early 1920s, modern greyhound racing was introduced into the United States. Smaller and lighter than show greyhounds, track greyhounds are selectively bred and usually stand between 25–29 inches tall and weigh 60–70 pounds. These dogs instinctively chase anything that moves quickly (as they are sighthounds, not bloodhounds), hence the *lure*—the mechanical hare they chase around the track. Greyhound racing is still a very popular spectator sport in the United States and, like horse racing, is enjoyed as a form of parimutuel gambling.

Greyhound racing is very controversial as the dogs experience little human contact and spend most of their non-racing time in crates. Once greyhounds are too old to race (somewhere between three and five years of age), many are euthanized, though there are now many rescue programs that find homes for retired racers. Because greyhounds are naturally docile and even-tempered, most adjust well to adoption and make wonderful pets.

The cover image is from *Cassell's Natural History*. The cover font is Adobe ITC Garamond. The text font is Linotype Birka; the heading font is Adobe Myriad Condensed; and the code font is LucasFont's TheSans Mono Condensed.

Related Titles from O'Reilly

Web Programming

ActionScript 3.0 Cookbook

ActionScript 3.0 Pocket Reference

ActionScript for Flash MX: The Definitive Guide, *2nd Edition*

Ajax Design Patterns

Ajax Hacks

Ajax on Rails

Building Scalable Web Sites

Dynamic HTML: The Definitive Reference, *3rd Edition*

Flash Hacks

Essential PHP Security

Google Advertising Tools

Google Hacks, *3rd Edition*

Google Map Hacks

Google Pocket Guide

Google: The Missing Manual, *2nd Edition*

Head First HTML with CSS & XHTML

Head Rush Ajax

HTTP: The Definitive Guide

JavaScript & DHTML Cookbook

JavaScript Pocket Reference, *2nd Edition*

JavaScript: The Definitive Guide, *5th Edition*

Learning PHP 5

Learning PHP and MySQL

PHP Cookbook, *2nd Edition*

PHP Hacks

PHP in a Nutshell

PHP Pocket Reference, *2nd Edition*

PHPUnit Pocket Guide

Programming ColdFusion MX, *2nd Edition*

Programming PHP, *2nd Edition*

Rails Cookbook

Rails in a Nutshell

Upgrading to PHP 5

Web Database Applications with PHP and MySQL, *2nd Edition*

Web Site Cookbook

Webmaster in a Nutshell, *3rd Edition*

Web Administration

Apache Cookbook

Apache Pocket Reference

Apache: The Definitive Guide, *3rd Edition*

Perl for Web Site Management

Squid: The Definitive Guide

Web Performance Tuning, *2nd Edition*

O'REILLY®